Jerusalem's Holy Places
and the Peace Process

Marshall J. Breger and Thomas A. Idinopulos

Policy Paper No. 46

THE WASHINGTON INSTITUTE FOR NEAR EAST POLICY

© 1998 by the Washington Institute for Near East Policy

Published in 1998 in the United States of America by the Washington Institute for Near East Policy, 1828 L Street N.W. Suite 1050, Washington, DC 20036

Library of Congress Cataloging-in-Publication Data

Breger, Marshall J., 1946-
    Jerusalem's holy places and the peace process / by Marshall J. Breger and Thomas A. Idinopulos.
        p. cm. — (Policy papers / Washington Institute for Near East Policy ; no. 46)
    Includes bibiliographical references (p.).
    ISBN 0-944029-73-6
    1. Jerusalem—International status. 2. Religion and politics—Jerusalem. 3. Arab–Israeli conflict—1993– 4. Jerusalem in Christianity. 5. Jerusalem in Islam. 6. Jerusalem in Judaism.
I. Idinopulos, Thomas A. II. Title. III. Series: Policy Papers (Washington Institute for Near East Policy) ; no. 46

DS109.94.B74 1998	97-31999
956.94'42--dc21	CIP

Cover design by Naylor Design Inc. Background cover photo of Jerusalem © Archive Photos/Neil Strassberg; inset photo of the Western Wall © Archive Photos; other inset photos courtesy of the Embassy of Israel, Washington, D.C.

The Authors

Marshall J. Breger is a visiting professor of law at the Catholic University of America. He served as solicitor of labor under President George Bush and as a special assistant to President Ronald Reagan. Before assuming his present position, he was a senior fellow at the Heritage Foundation in Washington, D.C. Professor Breger has written extensively on the Middle East. His most recent works include: "Understanding Jerusalem," *Middle East Quarterly* (March 1997); "Religion and Politics in Jerusalem," *Journal of International Affairs* (Summer 1996); "Jerusalem, Now and Then: The New Battle for Jerusalem," *Middle East Quarterly* (December 1994). He also writes a regular column for *Moment* magazine.

Thomas A. Idinopulos is a professor of religion at Miami University of Ohio. He has written numerous articles and books on religion and politics in the Middle East, including *Jerusalem Blessed, Jerusalem Cursed* (Chicago: Ivan R. Dee, 1991; Santiago, Chile: Andres Bello, 1997 [Spanish]). Most recently, he edited *The Sacred and the Scholars: Comparative Methodologies for the Study of Primary Religious Data* (Leiden, Netherlands: E. J. Brill, 1996), and authored *Land Weathered by Miracles: The History of Palestine from Bonaparte and Muhammad Ali to Ben-Gurion and the Mufti* (Chicago: Ivan R. Dee, forthcoming).

•   •   •

My mother, Beatrice Breger, died during the preparation of this manuscript. I dedicate this book to her—a person who always sought darchei shalom, *the ways of peace. May her memory be a blessing.*

— *Marshall J. Breger*

To Lea . . .
   With whom I discovered Jerusalem

— *Thomas A. Idinopulos*

"Even them will I bring to my holy mountain, and make them joyful in my house of prayer . . . for my house shall be called a house of prayer for all peoples."

Isaiah 56:7

"Glory be to Him Who made His servant to go on a night from the Sacred Mosque to the remote mosque of which We have blessed the precincts, so that We may show to him some of Our signs; surely He is the Hearing, the Seeing."

Qur'an 17:1

"The city on a hill cannot be hid."

Matthew 15:4

Contents

Acknowledgments

We thank Maria Pica, J.D., for creative and diligent research assistance. We are grateful to Prof. Silvio Ferrari in Milan; Dr. Eugene Fisher in Washington, D.C.; Moshe Hirsch in Jerusalem; Bill Hutman in Washington and Jerusalem; Prof. Ruth Lapidoth in Jerusalem; Prof. Charalambos Papastathis in Salonika; Prof. Yacov Reiter in Jerusalem; and Prof. Ifrah Zilberman in Jerusalem for their comments and suggestions. We thank as well Robert Satloff and the Washington Institute for Near East Policy for encouragement and support.

Preface

In the search for Arab–Israeli peace, "conventional wisdom" has long held that the thorniest issue for diplomats to resolve is the fate of Jerusalem and, for that reason, it belongs last on the agenda of negotiations. In recent years, some have offered the opposite argument: Since resolving Jerusalem is the *sine qua non* of any final peace agreement, it belongs on the top of the agenda, before all other issues. Whether first or last on the schedule of negotiations, as a May 1999 deadline looms for the expiration of the Oslo Accords and the completion of "final status talks," Jerusalem is sure to be at the center of debate over the next twelve months.

For the vast majority of Americans, who may view the larger Middle East conflict as a faraway concern, Jerusalem is special. Its history, its legacy, and its holiness connect ordinary people to the fate of the Arab–Israeli dispute like no other item on the negotiating agenda. Indeed, in the most fundamental way, most Americans have only two real interests in the content of a "final status" agreement between Israel and the Palestinians: that it live up to its promise to resolve all claims and terminate the conflict, once and for all, and that it maintain the unity and openness of the Holy City, with full access to the sites sacred to all religions.

How Israelis and Palestinians achieve those goals is their responsibility; America's role is not to impose solutions from afar. Indeed, The Washington Institute has refrained from publishing any studies offering "American answers" to items on the "final status" agenda precisely to avoid lending legitimacy to the idea that Americans should open that Pandora's Box.

This study, on the administration of Holy Places in Jerusalem, does not violate that basic principle. Instead, it analyzes more than four hundred years of Jerusalem's history to glean practical, operational lessons from the Ottoman, British, Jordanian, and Israeli control of the city and its holy sites: what has "worked" and what has not "worked." Thanks to the efforts of two recognized American scholars on Jerusalem this study offers a useful guide to negotiators, diplomats, and city planners on how to apply the constructive lessons of the past while attempting to avoid its mistakes.

We are confident that this study will be a useful tool in the hands of those committed to shaping a future for Jerusalem based on peace, openness, civility, and tolerance—qualities befitting the Holy City.

Mike Stein
President

Barbi Weinberg
Chairman

Executive Summary

The status of Jerusalem as a city filled with shrines, monuments, and other areas sacred to the Jewish, Christian, and Muslim faiths presents several problems to policymakers intent on pursuing Arab–Israeli peace. This book reviews past and present policies for administering and protecting the holy places and offers ten lessons policymakers should consider in framing future policy toward the holy places.

Historic Treatment of the Holy Places

Historically, one of the primary problems Jerusalem's rulers have faced is the difficulty in separating secular issues and concerns from religious ones. The city is a patchwork of religious communities and subcommunities whose claims over status and property often conflict. Under Ottoman rule, from 1517 to 1917, a religious foundation, or *waqf*, administered the Islamic holy places, but the fate of Christian and Jewish sites depended on those communities' standing with the Turkish caliphate, or Sublime Porte. As for Christian sites, the Ottomans often played off the competition among the Roman Catholic, Greek, Russian, and Armenian Orthodox Churches and the countries that supported them. In 1852, the Sublime Porte responded to the internal Christian disputes by decreeing a "status quo" among the Churches. With the Congress of Berlin in 1878, the great European powers agreed that "no alteration can be made in the status quo in the holy places," a decision that held until the fall of the Ottoman Empire during World War I. Jerusalem's Jews, however, lacked Great Power patronage altogether. Poor and powerless, they generally suffered high taxes and indignities at the hands of the Ottomans.

Palestine was placed under British Mandatory rule following the war. A Supreme Muslim Council administered the Muslim holy places, thus replacing or controlling the existing waqfs. Although generally supporting the Roman Catholic Church's claims, the Mandatory also pledged to uphold the Ottoman "status quo" and to keep close control of the holy places by declaring as final the high commissioner's judgment on disputes over the holy places. Increasing strife between Arabs and Jews led a Royal Commission in 1937 to recommend the partition of Palestine and the creation of a *corpus separatum* that would comprise Jerusalem, Bethlehem, and other sacred sites. Although never carried out, this recommendation became the basis for the 1947 United Nations Partition Resolution on Palestine.

This too was never fully carried out, as the Arab–Israeli war of 1948 led to the creation of a Jewish state in Palestine, the annexation by Jordan of what was to have been an independent Arab state in Palestine, and the division of Jerusalem between Israel and Jordan. Under Jordanian rule between 1948 and

1967, east Jerusalem's holy places, including the Old City and its ancient Jewish quarter, returned to a form of Ottoman-style protection. Christian sites were administered under a system in which each Church was free to follow its own laws but competed against other Churches for its right to the holy places. In contrast, the Jordanians turned a blind eye to desecration and looting of Jewish cemeteries, synagogues, schools, and homes in the Old City.

Since 1967, Israel has had complete control of Jerusalem and all its holy places. The Protection of Holy Places Law, approved by the Knesset soon after the war, defined Israel's approach to the administration of all the holy places that came under its jurisdiction: Christian, Muslim, as well as Jewish. In contrast to Jordanian prohibitions on Jewish worship at the Western Wall, this law permitted unfettered Muslim prayer in the Haram al-Sharif (Temple Mount) and permitted Christian Churches to acquire land and homes in Jerusalem. Israel's Ministry of Religious Affairs has since maintained effective contacts with the Christian community and responded to Christian needs. Concerning the Muslim population, since 1948 the waqf has administered Muslim sites in west Jerusalem, and its authority was extended in 1967 to east Jerusalem as well. A new Supreme Muslim Council was founded to protect Muslim rights, and, in certain respects, the waqf has had more autonomy under the Israelis that it did under British Mandatory rule.

Religious Concerns
Each religious community has its own interests, concerns, and problems. The Christian community's primary concerns are the affirmation of its rights and the assurance of access, freedom of activity, and pilgrimage to the Christian holy places. The community has three main problems. First, it is fractured and has many, sometimes conflicting, subcommunities. Second, many Christian lay residents are Palestinian, while most of the clergy are foreign (often European), and the two groups have different interests and needs. Finally, the Christian population is declining and many in the community fear that they will will lose their ability to speak up for Christian concerns.

The Muslim community is divided as well, in that both Jordan and the Palestinian Authority (PA) claim authority over the holy places. Jordan has said it will relinquish custodianship of the holy sites to the appropriate authority when the "final status" of the city is determined in negotiations, but King Hussein has made known that he envisions a long-term role for the Hashemites in the holy places, going so far as to suggest that the sites should be "above the sovereign considerations of any state." Thus Jordan continues to pay the salaries of religious functionaries in Jerusalem and has paid for renovations to al-Aqsa, although it cut its funding for West Bank religious institutions in 1994. The PA at that time created and began funding its own waqf bureaucracy, leading to the odd situation in which Jerusalem has two different waqf administrations, one Palestinian and one Jordanian. Practically speaking, this has not caused problems, as the PA minister of waqf and religious affairs, who is also the Supreme Muslim Council president, is Shaykh Hassan Tahboub, formerly a Jordanian waqf official. In other areas tensions have arisen, however: The PA and Jordan have each appointed different (and competing) directors of the al-Aqsa mosque.

Of special interest to both Jews and Muslims is the *Har HaBayit/Haram al-Sharif* (the "Temple Mount" in Hebrew, "Noble Enclosure" in Arabic). This area is a particular challenge as both religions lay special claim to it. Jews revere it as the site of the two Temples, with the Western Wall at the base of Har HaBayit being all that remains of them. Muslims built two of Islam's most treasured monuments on the mount: the Dome of the Rock shrine, the site of Muhammad's heavenly ascent, and the al-Aqsa mosque. Until the mid-nineteenth century, non-Muslims were barred from the area. Since 1967, non-Muslims have been allowed entry except during periods of Muslim prayer. Israeli law concerning the Har HaBayit/Haram is subtle and complex, as the country claims sovereignty but allows the waqf *de facto* control over day-to-day activity, consistent with considerations of public order. Many breakdowns of public order are caused by some ultra-Orthodox Jewish groups claiming a legal right to visit and pray on the Temple Mount, and the High Court of Jerusalem has decided myriad cases on this issue. Legally, Jews are allowed to visit and even to pray, but practically speaking, if they show any evidence of prayer they are physically removed (which is often the cause of the disturbances of public order). This has led some Jews to question what kind of "rights" they have if their prerogatives are regularly denied. Yet, most *haredi* or ultra-Orthodox Jews do not believe Jews should be near the Temple Mount anyway, for fear of accidental desecration; they believe the reestablishment of prayer on the Temple Mount should be left to Messianic times.

Proposals for Administering Jerusalem and the Holy Places

More than sixty proposals for the solution of the Jerusalem problem have been made since the Sykes–Picot Agreement of 1916, each of which recommends guarantees for the security of the holy places. Generally, these proposals can be divided into two groups: those that propose that Jerusalem should remain undivided under Israeli sovereignty, and those that propose that the city should be physically or politically separated under dual or shared Israeli and Palestinian control.

Public opinion polls show that the Israeli people overwhelmingly favor the first kind of solution, often with some provision for the political representation of Arab Jerusalemites and the "Vaticanization" of the Muslim sites. The PA's current position falls into the second category: that Jerusalem be physically undivided but politically separated with dual or shared sovereignty. Yet the Old City, with its close neighborhoods and shrines, poses problems under this solution that are usually met by subproposals giving Jews control over the Jewish Quarter, Muslims control of the Muslim Quarter, and allowing Christians to decide between Jewish and Muslim sovereignty. These subproposals in turn face heavy criticism for their political utopianism.

Administrative solutions, which deal solely with the holy places and not questions of Jerusalem's sovereignty or political determination, are of three sorts. The first would create an interfaith committee of Muslim, Christian, and Jewish representatives to administer the holy sites; this solution is akin to League of Nations and UN proposals first for a special commission and later for a *corpus separatum*. The second solution would devolve control over a religion's holy sites, in a sort of "functional internationalization," to committees comprising members of that faith. This is easier said than done, however. The third approach would leave the matter to various international guarantees such as the UN Educational, Scientific, and Cultural Organization (UNESCO) and Hague Conventions. As Israel already subscribes to many of these guarantees, reaffirming its commitment to the protection of the holy places and their respective religious communities' rights would be both a simple and unilateral matter.

Ten Lessons

According to the Oslo Accords, "Jerusalem" is an item in the agenda of Israeli–Palestinian final status talks. The administration of holy places is an important element within the overall set of Jerusalem-related issues. The legacy of Ottoman, British, Jordanian, and Israeli control of these sites over the past five centuries offers useful lessons to guide both the negotiations and the leaders of the various communities who determine the religious mosaic of Jerusalem on a daily basis.

1. Following the dictum that "good fences make good neighbors," the three religious communities' quarters, compounds, and neighborhoods should be respected as belonging to specific people following specific lifestyles.

2. Extending the "good fences" doctrine to Jerusalem's holy places, the guidelines governing control over and access to holy sites should be clear and well-understood by all communities.

3. Undergirding that same principle, symbolic rhetoric should not be allowed to get in the way of practical management of the holy places; to that end, functional sovereignty may be a particularly useful solution.

4. Freedom of worship is only abstract unless access is provided to holy places for worship; the issue is not who owns a site, but how the site can be administered to provide public access while respecting community traditions.

5. Mechanisms should be structured to allow Israeli rabbinical and political officials to meet with leaders of the major faiths on the basis of dignity and equality.

6. Israel need not and should not wait for a comprehensive settlement to

move to improve its political and moral agenda regarding the holy places.

7. Waqf officials should refrain from using religious services on the Haram to incite violence. Also, religious leaders, especially those appointed by political authorities, have special responsibility to reject incitement and to promote intercommunal tolerance. In this respect, the PA should preclude any individual from concurrently holding the positions of the head of the Supreme Muslim Council and the PA minister of religious affairs.

8. The Christian communities need to clarify their goals and needs in a concrete manner to present a more united voice.

9. It is important to resist the hallowing of new "holy places" whenever possible, a lesson that is easy to state yet hard to follow.

10. Each religious group should try to clarify for itself and for the benefit of the other groups what it considers the "holy" boundaries of "its" Jerusalem.

Explanation of Citations

Many of the citations in this book come from international legal sources. To assist readers interested in searching for them, the authors have compiled the following guide to acronyms and page references.

ICJ Reports   Published Reports of the International Court of Justice

LSI   Laws of the State of Israel

UNTS   United Nations Treaty Series
cited as {volume} UNTS {page number}
ex.: 249 UNTS 240

HCJ   Supreme Court of Israel, sitting as a High Court of Justice
cited as HCJ {case number}/{year}
ex.: HCJ 4185/90

PD   *Piskay Din*, the published reports of judgments by the Supreme Court of Israel
cited as {volume} ({part}) PD {page} ({year})
ex.: 24(2) PD 141 (1970)

I

Introduction

As a city filled with "sacred space," Jerusalem poses several problems for policymakers seeking a political solution to the Israeli–Palestinian conflict. Any solution to the challenge of finding an agreed upon settlement must promise to protect the holy places—the "sacred space" of Judaism, Christianity, and Islam.

Yet, history does not tell a hopeful tale. Upon capturing the holy city, conqueror after conqueror defiled Jerusalem's holy places. There were, of course, some notable exceptions. On conquering Jerusalem in 638, following Muslim tradition, Caliph Umar refused to pray in the Christian holy places, knowing that if he entered a church to pray his followers would destroy it. And Lord Edmund Allenby, on entering the city in 1917 after Britain won control over Palestine from the defunct Ottoman Empire, took pains to dismount and enter on foot as a pilgrim rather than as a conqueror (in marked contrast to Germany's Kaiser Wilhelm, whose progress through the city in 1898 required the Jaffa gate to be widened for his chariot).

The goals of this paper are to identify the role of Jerusalem's holy places in the ongoing Arab–Israeli peace process. In pursuing this goal we will comment on the recent past history of Jerusalem's holy places as seen through successive Ottoman, British, and Jordanian administrations. We will also look at Israel's unification of Jerusalem in 1967 and the resulting legal issues surrounding Jerusalem and the administration of the holy places.

Jerusalem's status as a holy city necessarily implicates the interests of Christian, Islamic, and Jewish communities with the city and outside of Israel. We will identify the interests of each community with particular emphasis on the competing claims of Jews and Muslims over the status of the Temple Mount. Fractures within a community, the need of a group to maintain its presence in Jerusalem, and the groups' dealings with one another often complicate these divergent interests.

We next turn to an examination of past and future proposals for Jerusalem and the holy places. In each of these proposals, which range widely and encompass numerous methods of splitting control—if not sovereignty—of the city of Jerusalem, one seemingly irreconcilable aspect of the problem has been the issue of the holy places.

Our review of the historical, political, and religious interests in Jerusalem and the holy places leads us to suggest ten lessons to be learned from this history. We offer these lessons not as the formula for any ultimate resolution, but as a basis for developing practical solutions that will protect the holy places and Jerusalem itself for future generations.

The reader should note that by "holy places" we are referring to more than the principal shrines that symbolize the Jewish, Christian, and Muslim presence in Jerusalem.[1] World attention focuses on the Western Wall, the Church of the Holy Sepulcher, the Dome of the Rock, and other important shrines. Yet, a more complete understanding of holy places must also focus on the hundreds of mosques, synagogues, churches, monasteries, and cemeteries scattered all about Jerusalem.[2] Indeed, so much of the city's land is explicitly sacred to one community or another that Jerusalem well deserves its title, "Holy City."

It is not our aim in this paper to determine whether or how much Jerusalem is a holy city to Jews, Christians, or Muslims. Nor do we intend to discuss the question of which of these three religious communities has superior spiritual or historical claims on Jerusalem, its holy places, or any part of the city. We assume that Jerusalem is holy in definite but different ways to Jews, Christians, and Muslims, and that specific places in the city are recognized holy places for each of the three communities. Our concern is to uncover the roots of the problems generating conflict over Jerusalem's holy places and to describe possible solutions to these problems in relation to the current peace process. We hope that this essay can contribute in some small way to the resolution of these conflicts.

---

[1] We do not here attempt an analytic definition of what constitutes a holy or sacred space, but instead accept traditional listings such as those compiled by the United Nations in 1949. These include Christian holy sites such as the Church of the Holy Sepulcher enclosing Jesus' tomb; the Churches of St. Anne, St. James, and St. Mark; the Tomb of the Virgin; the Garden of Gethsemane; and the Basilica of the Nativity in Bethlehem. Jewish holy sites listed include the Western Wall, Rachel's tomb, Jewish tombs in the Kidron Valley, and the Jewish cemetery on the Mount of Olives. Muslim holy sites such as the mosques on the Haram al-Sharif; the Tomb of David (Nebi Da'ud); the western wall of the Haram, known to Muslims as al-Buraq; and the Mosque of the Ascension are among those on the UN's list. See "Central Portion of the Jerusalem Area: Principle Holy Places," *United Nations Map* no. 229 (November 1949); see also Elihu Lauterpacht, *Jerusalem and the Holy Places* (London: The Anglo–Israel Association, 1968), p. 5, note 1. For a discussion of "holy places," as detailed in the Ottoman "status quo," see L. G. A. Cust, *The Status Quo in the Holy Places* (London: His Majesty's Stationery Office, 1929; reproduced in Jerusalem: Ariel Publishing House, 1980), p. 12. It is worth noting that in "no Israeli law, nor in any Mandatory law is there any definition of the term" holy places; see Shmuel Berkowitz, *The Holy Places in Jerusalem: Legal Aspects* (Part II) *Justice* no. 12 (1997) p. 21.

For a discussion of the meaning of sacred space, see Larry E. Shiner, "Sacred Space, Profane Space, Human Space," *Journal of the American Academy of Religion* 35 (December 1972), pp. 425–436.

[2] Whereas we recognize that the question of classification is itself controversial, we limit ourselves to a consensus meaning of a holy place and do not, for example, include religious schools. Thus, we deem the question of whether a Muslim school in the Old City will be run by Israel, Jordan, or the Palestinian Authority (PA) to be more a political matter than a religious one.

II

Historical Setting

In his influential monograph, *Jerusalem and the Holy Places*, Elihu Lauterpacht states, "Linking Jerusalem and the holy places tends to promote . . . confusion . . . For in truth there exist two quite distinct problems—the question of the holy places and the question of Jerusalem."[1] This view has generally been held by each Israeli government since 1967 and was reflected in the oft-repeated view of the 1993–96 Labor government that the status of Jerusalem "is closed politically and open religiously."[2] Israeli prime minister Binyamin Netanyahu, in a January 1997 meeting with Pope John Paul, reiterated this view in stating, "We are ready to give guarantees to Christians and Muslims, but we do not intend to discuss the [city's] political sovereignty."[3]

In contrast, our study and field work suggest that the problems of Jerusalem and the holy places can be distinguished but not separated nor discussed as "quite distinct problems." We do not mean to suggest that the city should not remain united or under Israeli sovereignty, but merely that, for several reasons, the issues that undergird conflict in the holy places cannot be dealt with outside the larger questions of control and autonomy of the city itself.[4]

First, Jerusalem cannot be separated from the holy places because in Jerusalem, politics cannot be separated from religion (consider the secular–*haredi* debate in Israel and its effect on Jerusalem's politics). Jerusalem is not a western European or American city that has experienced the separation of secular functions from sacred practices. Although the municipal government of Jerusalem administers public services, the government, administration, and laws of Jerusalem are so intertwined with religious interests and parties as to render porous the traditional distinction between the secular and the sacred. In Jerusalem, religion cannot be extricated from the public square.

Second, any careful study of Jerusalem will show that the city should be understood as a patchwork of Jewish, Christian, and Muslim ethnoreligious communities and subcommunities, each of which has religiopolitical interests

---

[1] Elihu Lauterpacht, *Jerusalem and the Holy Places* (London: Anglo–Israel Association, 1968), p. 5.

[2] "Peres: Israel Open on Status of Moslem, Christian Holy Places in Jerusalem," *Jerusalem Post*, July 13, 1994, p. 2.

[3] "Netanyahu to Tell Pope that Jerusalem Stays United," *Reuters,* January 28, 1997.

[4] Each author may in fact have a different view on the matter of future sovereignty over Jerusalem as a city.

and claims and many of which come into conflict when questions of status, property, and privilege are raised.[5] These interests and claims intensify when the question of holy places is raised. For each group, the holy places are the symbolic focus of communal self-identity and worship, ethnic pride, and national ambition.

And finally, just as one cannot separate the holy places from Jerusalem's religious communities, so one cannot separate the holy places from Jerusalem itself. Every question affecting Jerusalem's holy places is both sacred and secular, religious and political, spiritual and national. This is what makes the study of Jerusalem's holy places both so complicated and so challenging. For surely there can be no effective future peace between Israelis and Palestinians if the holy places continue to be the flashpoints of intercommunal tensions and bloody divisions.

To gain a better perspective on workable solutions, we will now examine the policies of the successive governments that have attempted to deal with the conflict surrounding the holy places during their rule of Jerusalem.[6]

OTTOMAN PERIOD, 1517–1917

As an Islamic power, the Ottoman government ruling Palestine and Jerusalem for 400 years had no need to legislate concerning Islamic holy places because those places were administered by a *waqf* (religious foundation) recognized in *shari'a* (Muslim law).[7]

It was a different matter for the holy places of Jews and Christians. Until the legal "equality" reforms of the mid-nineteenth century, Jews and Christians had secure but secondary status in the Ottoman empire. Defined as *dhimmi*s (protected ones) under Muslim law and prohibited from carrying arms, Jews and Christians were required to pay the *jizya* (a special tax) to ensure their personal

---

[5] See Michael Romann and Alex Weingrod, *Living Together Separately: Arabs and Jews in Contemporary Jerusalem* (Princeton, N.J.: Princeton University Press, 1991).

[6] Among the studies used in this and other historical sections of the paper are M. A. Aamiry, *Jerusalem: Arab Origin and Heritage* (London: Longman, 1978); K. J. Asali, ed., *Jerusalem in History* (New York: Olive Branch Press, 1978); Yehoshua Ben-Arieh, *Jerusalem in the Nineteenth Century: The Old City* (New York: St. Martin's Press, 1984); John Gray, *A History of Jerusalem* (London: Robert Hale, 1969); Thomas A. Idinopulos, *Jerusalem Blessed, Jerusalem Cursed: Jews, Christians, and Muslims in the Holy City from David's Time to Our Own* (Chicago: Ivan R. Dee, 1991); F. E. Peters, *Jerusalem: The Holy City in the Eyes of Chroniclers: Visitors, Pilgrims, and Prophets from the Days of Abraham to the Beginnings of Modern Times* (Princeton, N.J.: Princeton University Press, 1985).

[7] The *waqf* is a form of trust, the usufruct of which is designated for a particular beneficiary; in the case of a religious waqf, the beneficiary is usually a mosque. According to the majority opinion, the corpus of the waqf becomes the property of God. See *Encyclopedia of Religion* 15, s.v. *"waqf,"* Mircea Eliade, ed. (New York: MacMillan, 1987), pp. 337–339; *Oxford Encyclopedia of the Modern Islamic World* 14, s.v. *"waqf,"* John L. Esposito, ed. (New York: Oxford University Press, 1995), pp. 312–316.

protection. The dhimmi status of Jews and Christians directly affected how Ottoman authorities viewed and treated Jewish and Christian holy sites.

Through the centuries Jews and Christians suffered excessive taxes and contemptuous treatment at the hands of Muslim officials and people. During the nineteenth and early twentieth centuries, Jerusalem's Jews, powerless and poor, experienced indignities directed at them by Muslims as the Jews conducted their worship at the Wall—indignities such as stoning, herding animals in the narrow alley before the Wall, and befouling the sacred Wall with animal excrement.[8] In the late nineteenth century wealthy Jewish philanthropists, led by Baron Edmond de Rothschild, attempted to purchase the Mugrabi Quarter facing the Wall, but the Muslim waqf officials demanded an exorbitant price.

Likewise, Christians in Jerusalem complained that during periods of military conflict, Muslims made a practice of defacing the figures of saints in churches. As the Ottoman Empire entered the modern age and as the reform movement took root in the mid-nineteenth century, charges against Muslim desecration of Christian holy sites were replaced by complaints about Muslim financial and political exploitation of Christian and Jewish holy sites.

For centuries Ottoman emperors financially exploited the Christian holy places. The keen competition between the Latin (Roman Catholic), Greek, Russian, and Armenian Orthodox Churches—and the European nations supporting them—for control of the holy places made them convenient targets for Ottoman exploitation. To enhance its relations with Venice or France or Russia, the Ottoman government, or Sublime Porte, made a practice of selling, to the highest bidder, preeminent worship rights at the Churches of the Holy Sepulcher and Nativity.[9] In some instances, one church community would lose a valued property to another community because it could not pay the Ottoman taxes. In this way, Jerusalem's Monastery of the Cross, which Christian tradition venerates as the site of the tree from which Jesus' cross was cut, passed from the Georgian Orthodox to the Greek Orthodox Church.

In a decree of 1740, the Ottoman government, anxious for French military and political support, turned its back on its loyal Greek subjects and conferred on the Latin Church preeminent rights at the shrines in Jerusalem and Bethlehem. The Greeks were furious. In the Church of the Holy Sepulcher, Greek and

---

[8] The controversy over the Western Wall, culminating in the riot and massacre of 1929, is discussed in Yehoshua Porath, *The Emergence of the Palestinian Arab National Movement, 1918–1929* (London: Frank Cass, 1974), pp. 258–273. For a differing assessment of this controversy, see Philip Mattar, *The Mufti of Jerusalem: Al-Hajj Amin al-Husayni and the Palestinian National Movement* (New York: Columbia University Press, 1988), pp. 33–49. See also Pinhas Ofer, "The Commission on the Palestinian Disturbances of August 1929: Appointment, Terms of Reference, Procedure and Report," *Middle Eastern Studies* 25, no. 3 (1985), pp. 349–361; Martin Kolinsky, "Premeditation in the Palestinian Disturbances of August 1929," *Middle Eastern Studies* 26, no. 1 (1990), pp. 18–34.

[9] Ben-Arieh, *Jerusalem in the Nineteenth Century,* pp. 184–264.

Franciscan monks attacked each other with candlesticks and crosses. To Ottoman officials caught in the middle, the internal stability of the empire suddenly posed a greater challenge than cultivating relations with Catholic France. A new decree in 1757 restored to the Greeks preeminent rights in the holy places.

In 1850, the disappearance of the silver star in the Grotto of the Nativity in Bethlehem stirred the ever-boiling pot of inter-Christian resentment and provoked the Crimean War. The Latin inscription on the star persuaded the Franciscans that the Greeks had stolen it, while the latter accused the Franciscans of removing it so they could blame the Greeks. As accusations flew, France seized the opportunity to demand that the Ottoman authorities return the rights and privileges at the shrines guaranteed by the Sultan to the Catholic Church in 1740. Russia vigorously protested any change that would prejudice the interests of Greek and other Eastern Orthodox Christians. The Turks, seeing a chance to slip out of past obligations, announced that they were withdrawing "protector" status from both France and Russia. At the height of the crisis, the Sultan issued the *firman* (decree) of status quo in 1852, which fixed the rights and responsibilities of the different churches as regards the holy places.[10] The resulting imbroglio drew all the European powers into the Crimean War.

Continuing unrest in the Ottoman Empire led Europe's great powers to convene the Congress of Berlin in 1878. The resulting Treaty of Berlin decreed that "no alteration can be made in the status quo in the holy places." It was a prudent decision. The quarrels between Greek and Latin Churches had drawn in the great nations of Europe—to their regret—and they were now looking for ways to end the cycle of destructive confrontation with one another.

Unfortunately, they failed. The Treaty of Berlin froze the question of Christian holy places, but after the collapse of the Ottoman Empire following World War I, European nations again confronted one another over Palestine and the whole Middle East. Although the victorious allies viewed the demise of the Ottoman Empire as a chance to enlarge colonial spheres of influence, new forces of Zionism and Arab nationalism were stirring, each with its own sense of sacred space and each with a powerful resentment of how the other had desecrated it.[11]

BRITISH RULE, 1917–1948

Upon conquering Jerusalem on December 9, 1917, the British set about governing capital and country with a sense of historic obligation and high moral purpose. This was seen in the speech made by General Edmund Allenby when he

---

[10] For a discussion of the "status quo," see L. G. A. Cust, *The Status Quo in the Holy Places,* and Walter Zander, *Israel and the Holy Places of Christendom* (New York: Praeger, 1971).

[11] No better study of World War I and its aftermath in the Middle East exists than David Fromkin, *A Peace to End All Peace: The Fall of the Ottoman Empire and the Creation of the Modern Middle East* (New York: Henry Holt, 1989).

took control of the Holy City. The last words of the speech showed that the holiness of Jerusalem was uppermost in the government's mind:

> Since your city is regarded with affection by the adherents of three of the great religions of mankind, and its soil has been consecrated by the prayers and pilgrimages of multitudes of devout people of these three religions for many centuries, therefore do I make known to you that every sacred building, monument, holy spot, traditional shrine, endowment, pious bequest, or customary place of prayer of whatsoever form of the three religions, will be maintained and protected according to the existing customs and beliefs of those to whose faiths they are sacred. [12]

Britain's obligations toward the holy places were later defined in the League of Nations Mandate, ratified in 1923.[13] Article 13 of the Mandate reads,

> All responsibility in connection with the holy places and religious buildings or sites in Palestine, including that of preserving existing rights and of securing free access to the holy places, religious buildings and sites, and the free exercise of worship, while ensuring the requirements of public order and decorum, is assumed by the Mandatory, who shall be responsible solely to the League of Nations.[14]

The special sensitivity felt by Britain as a Christian power governing Muslim endowments was expressed in the closing words of article 13: "[N]othing in this Mandate shall be construed as conferring upon the Mandatory authority to interfere with the fabric or the management of purely Muslim sacred shrines, the immunities of which are guaranteed."[15] To meet Muslim concerns for autonomy in their religious affairs, the British, in 1921, created a Supreme Muslim Council (SMC)[16] thus giving the SMC "unqualified," if *de facto*, control of Islamic waqfs in Palestine.[17]

---

[12] W. T. Massey, *How Jerusalem Was Won, Being the Record of Allenby's Campaign in Palestine* (London: Constable and Co., Ltd., 1919), p. 286.

[13] *Mandate for Palestine, together with a note by the Secretary-General to its Application to the Territory of Trans-Jordan*, League of Nations, Cmd. 1785, December 1922, in Ruth Lapidoth and Moshe Hirsch, eds., *The Arab–Israel Conflict and its Resolution: Selected Documents* (Boston: Martinus Nijhoff Publishers, 1991), pp. 25–32. Prior to the League's involvement, Palestine had been ruled by a military government.

[14] Ibid., p. 28. Article 9 proclaimed that the religious interests of "the various peoples and communities shall be fully guaranteed." The article also ensured that "the control and administration of waqfs be exercised in accordance with religious law and the disposition of the founders." Ibid., p. 27.

[15] Ibid., p. 28.

[16] British efforts at preserving this autonomy were manifested in several policies that entrusted the administration of the Haram to the SMC; allowed the SMC to charge non-Muslims admission to the Haram; and, placed security at the site in the hands of the waqf administration. These policies were never embodied in legislation; rather, they were implemented in consideration of British relations with the Muslim community. Yitzhak Reiter, *Islamic Institutions in Jerusalem* (London: Kluwer Law International, 1997), p. 89.

[17] Ibid., pp. 4–5. See also Yitzhak Reiter, *Islamic Endowments in Jerusalem under British Mandate* (London: Frank Cass, 1996), pp. 17–47; Uri M. Kupferschmidt, *The Supreme Muslim Council:*

A turning point in Jerusalem's Arab politics came around 1920 when the Mandatory government made several decisions that enhanced the power of the Jerusalem Muslim aristocracy led by the Husayni clan, the least moderate of the Muslim family elites.[18] A young member of the Husayni clan, al-Hajj Amin al-Husayni, was maneuvered by the British High Commissioner, Sir Herbert Samuel, into the newly created religious position of Grand Mufti of Jerusalem and Palestine. In 1922, the Mandatory appointed Amin president of the newly created SMC, responsible for representing the Muslim affairs of Palestine to the Mandatory government.

The local balance of power was thus tipped in favor of the Husaynis, who now controlled the appointment of judges to the shari'a courts, commanded the finances of the waqf, and had enormous status and influence with the Mandatory government. In the fifteen years that Amin held power, he made the waqf treasury a personal bank to fight Zionism as well as to promote the religious importance of Jerusalem and its holy places throughout the Islamic world.

Mufti Amin used his office to engage in extremist politics that ultimately proved destructive to both Palestinian nationalist goals and to any possible cooperation between Arabs and Jews. His campaign of vilification against Jerusalem's Jewish community was particularly vicious.[19] He accused Jews of plotting to use their presence at the Wall eventually to seize the Haram and its mosques. Amin's inflammatory rhetoric contributed to the 1929 riots and had attendant consequences for the future of Arab–Jewish relations in the Mandatory.

Mandatory officials had more success with the Christian population of Jerusalem. Officials encouraged the development of native Arab churches, particularly Anglican adherents, and tackled the financial problems of the large and influential Greek Orthodox Church. Their support of traditional Roman Catholic privileges and powers reassured France, the principal European defender of Latin interests in the Holy Land. By endorsing the Ottoman Empire's 1852 firman of status quo, the British government showed it would not play one church off against the other.[20]

Islam under British Mandate for Palestine (Leiden, Netherlands: E. J. Brill, 1987). This autonomy continued until the Arab riots of 1937, when the British began to intervene "to a much greater extent in *waqf* affairs" (Yitzhak Reiter, *Islamic Endowments*, p. 26). Michael Dumper, an English academic with a Palestinian perspective, goes even further, stating that after 1937, "[t]he British, in effect, took over the administration of the *waqfs* [sic] themselves." Michael Dumper, *The Politics of Jerusalem since 1967* (New York: Columbia University Press, 1997), p. 47.

[18] For an account of British Mandatory policy affecting Jerusalem's Muslim elites, see Joel S. Migdal, *Palestinian Society and Politics* (Princeton, N.J.: Princeton University Press, 1980), pp. 19–31.

[19] For differing assessments of the career of al-Hajj Amin al-Husayni, see Yehoshua Porath, *The Emergence of the Palestinian Arab National Movement,* and Philip Mattar, *The Mufti of Jerusalem.*

[20] For Mandatory policy affecting Jerusalem's Christian holy places, see Walter Zander, *Israel and the Holy Places of Christendom*, pp. 55–71.

To keep close control of the administration of the holy places, including the Western Wall, the High Commission in 1924 determined that "no cause or matter in connection with the holy places or religious buildings or sites in Palestine or the rights or claims relating to different religious communities in Palestine shall be heard or determined by any court in Palestine."[21] According to this Order in Council, the High Commissioner's decisions were final and binding on all parties. Issues related to the holy places were reserved for the political realm, not the court system.

Many of the conflicts currently raised by the Jewish claims to worship at the Temple Mount[22] were presaged by similar disputes during the Mandate over Jewish prayer at the Western (then Wailing) Wall. Indeed the 1929 riots, which would become a watershed for both Zionism and Arab nationalism, were triggered in large part by disputes over Jewish rights at the Western Wall. After the riots, which resulted in the massacre of 116 Arabs and 232 Jews in several cities, the Mandatory authority set up an investigative commission (the Shaw Commission) to examine their cause.[23] The Shaw Commission recommended that the League of Nations appoint an *ad hoc* commission "to determine the rights and claims connected with the Wailing Wall."[24] The League then asked the British government to appoint on its behalf an international commission of three persons of non-British nationality to examine the matter. The International Commission on the Wailing Wall—consisting of a Swedish, a Dutch, and a Swiss national—spent one month holding hearings in Palestine. Rejecting the Arab view that the Jews had no rights of access or worship at the Wall, the international commission gave Jews untrammeled access to the Wall, but laid down severe restrictions for Jewish worship precluding Jews, for example, from placing "appurtenances of worship" (such as an ark containing Torah scrolls) near the Wall on all but specific holy days.[25] The resulting rules regulating Jewish worship at the Wall became the responsibility of the office of the Chief Rabbinate established by the Mandatory authority.[26]

---

[21] See the *Palestine (Holy Places) Order in Council* of 1924, in L. G. A. Cust, *The Status Quo in the Holy Places* (Jerusalem: Ariel Publishing House, 1980), pp. 65–66.

[22] Our use of the terms Temple Mount or Har HaBayit is not meant to denigrate Muslim claims to the Haram. We use these terms interchangeably, according to context.

[23] See *Report of the Commission on the Palestine Disturbances of August 1929*, Cmd. 3530, (London: His Majesty's Stationery Office, March 1930).

[24] Ibid., p. 157. See also Meron Benvenisti, *City of Stone: The Hidden History of Jerusalem* (Berkeley: University of California Press, 1996), p. 81.

[25] See *The Palestine (Western or Wailing Wall) Order in Council*, 1931, in Moses Doukhan, ed., *Laws of Palestine 1926–1931* 4, (Tel Aviv: L. M. Rotenberg, 1933), p. 1484.

[26] *Report of the Commission appointed by His Majesty's Government in the United Kingdom of Great Britain and Northern Ireland, with the approval of the Council of the League of Nations, to determine the rights and claims of Moslems and Jews in connection with the Western or Wailing Wall at Jerusalem (International Commission for the Wailing Wall), December 1930* (London: His

From the riots of 1929 to the outbreak of the Arab rebellion in 1936, Mandatory officials found themselves caught in the middle of increasingly violent hostilities between Arabs and Jews. This civil strife led to a major policy reassessment by Britain. In 1937, a Royal [Peel] Commission Report called for the partition of Palestine to allow for the creation of independent Arab and Jewish states.[27] One of the more significant provisos of the Royal Commission's recommendation affected Jerusalem and its holy places. The report stated, "The partition of Palestine is subject to the overriding necessity of keeping the sanctity of Jerusalem and Bethlehem inviolate and of ensuring free and safe access to them for all the world."[28] Safeguarding the holy places was considered, in the words of the Mandate, "a sacred trust of civilization."[29] Accordingly, the members of the Royal Commission proposed that Jerusalem, Bethlehem, Nazareth, and the Sea of Galilee (Lake Tiberias) be made a *corpus separatum* and thus be detached from the proposed Arab and Jewish states. With a designated road access to the sea, the Christian holy areas would have the status of a separate enclave under international administration.[30]

The Royal Commission recommendation on the partition of Palestine was never carried out. The British White Paper of 1939 (involving major concessions to Arab political demands)[31] and the events of World War II preoccupied policymakers. In the years following the conclusion of the European war in 1945, Arab–Jewish relations in Palestine once again degener-ated into open mutual violence. The British Labour government, led by Prime Minister Clement Attlee and Foreign Minister Ernest Bevin, sought a way to extricate Britain from a situation that was costing Britain heavily in lives, money, and moral prestige. In

---

Majesty's Stationery Office, 1931). Although generally favorable to the Muslim position in this controversy, a useful summary of the International Commission's findings can be found in A. L. Tibawi, *The Islamic Pious Foundations in Jerusalem: Origins: History and Usurpation by Israel* (London: Islamic Cultural Centre, 1978), pp. 27–29.

[27] See *Palestine Royal Commission Report,* Cmd. 5479, (London: His Majesty's Stationery Office, July 1937); see also *Palestine Statement of Policy by His Majesty's Government in the United Kingdom,* Cmd. 5513, (London: His Majesty's Stationary Office, July 1937).

[28] *Palestine Royal Commission Report,* p. 381.

[29] See *Article 22 of the Covenant of the League of Nations,* in Lapidoth and Hirsch, *The Arab–Israel Conflict,* pp. 23-25. Yet, as one later case noted, "[N]o technical significance can be attached to the words 'sacred trust of civilization.'" *International Status of South West Africa,* Advisory Opinion of July 11, 1950, ICJ Reports 1950, p. 148 (Lord Arnold McNair, separate opinion).

[30] *Palestine Royal Commission Report,* pp. 382–384, and accompanying Map no. 8. The Royal Commission's reluctance to entrust the Christian holy places to Muslim or Jewish governing authorities reflects the tragedy of historical experience. The continual past dispossession or desecration of holy places has made Jewish, Christian, and Muslim communities utterly distrustful of any party commitments to govern the holy places wisely and fairly.

[31] John Marlowe, *The Seat of Pilate, An Account of the Palestine Mandate* (London: Cresset Press, 1959), pp. 157–159; see also, *British Statesmen on the White Paper* (New York: American Zionist Bureau, 1939), as it contains speeches made before Parliament.

early 1947, the decision was reached to resign the Mandate and to ask the United Nations to address itself to the future disposition of Palestine.

In November 1947, after much hard lobbying by Zionists, who favored partition, and Arab leaders, who opposed it, the United Nations General Assembly voted in favor of partitioning Palestine into independent Arab and Jewish states. Guided by the recommendation of the earlier Royal Commission, the Jerusalem–Bethlehem area (with a corridor to the Mediterranean sea) was designated a *corpus separatum* to be administered by the UN itself.

Once again, events overwhelmed diplomacy. The UN recommendation on partitioning Palestine was not acted upon because of the outbreak of war in May 1948 between the newly declared State of Israel and five surrounding Arab nations.

Yet, the 1947 UN Partition Resolution on Palestine proved to be an influential document.[32] Those who support the internationalization of Jerusalem, or those who feel that the holy places can be secure only under an international regime, continually turn to it for support. Linking the Christian holy places to the internationalization of Jerusalem (as the Roman Catholic Church did until 1968)[33] also gives a powerful argument to those who oppose Israel's unilateral act of naming Jerusalem as its sovereign capital, as well as the extension of Israeli sovereignty into mainly Arab-populated eastern Jerusalem.

Clearly, the UN resolution of 1947 is a benchmark on Jerusalem and the holy places. Its relevance to future events, however, has likely diminished over time. Support for internationalization has clearly ebbed. As a practical matter, the U.S. government abandoned internationalization after the June 1967 War (although it still remained "on the books").[34] The Vatican, as this paper will later discuss, stopped promoting internationalization even before its signing of the Vatican–Israel Accord in 1993. At this time, the internationalization option is simply not on the political agenda of any of the "stakeholders" in the Jerusalem dispute.

---

[32] See United Nations General Assembly (UNGA) *Resolution 181 (II) on the Future Government of Palestine*, November 29, 1947, in Ruth Lapidoth and Moshe Hirsch, eds., *The Jerusalem Question and its Resolution: Selected Documents* (Boston: Martinus Nijhoff Publishers, 1994), pp. 6–10.

[33] Silvio Ferrari and Francesco Margiotta Broglio, "The Vatican, the European Community, and the status of Jerusalem," *Studi in Memoria di Mario Condorelli* 1, no. 1 (Milan: Dott. A. Giuffrè Editore, 1988), pp. 579–580. For a useful discussion of the past Vatican position on Jerusalem (internationalization of the whole city) and the present position ("special status," and "international guarantees"), see Silvio Ferrari, "The Religious Significance of Jerusalem in the Middle East Peace Process: Some Legal Implications," *Catholic University Law Review 45* (1996), p. 733; Silvio Ferrari, "The Struggle for Jerusalem," *European Journal of International Affairs* 11 (1991), pp. 22–39; Silvio Ferrari, "The Vatican, Israel, and the Jerusalem Question (1943–1984)," *Middle East Journal* 39, no. 2 (Spring 1985), pp. 316–331.

[34] Marshall J. Breger, "Jerusalem Now and Then: The New Battle for Jerusalem," *Middle East Quarterly* (December 1994), p. 27. The evolving American position is developed in Yossi Feintuch, *U.S. Policy on Jerusalem* (Westport, Conn.: Greenwood Press, 1987).

JORDANIAN RULE IN EASTERN JERUSALEM, 1948–1967

The Arab–Israeli war of 1948 had a dramatic impact on Jerusalem and the holy places. As a consequence of the war, Israel gained the Jewish-inhabited New City of Jerusalem but lost control of the Old City and its ancient Jewish Quarter to Jordan.

Jews had reason to mourn the loss of the Jewish Quarter. No sooner had the original inhabitants been moved out (and ultimately repatriated), than Arab soldiers looted synagogues, schools, and homes and made a fire of religious articles. Acting under orders, Arab soldiers dynamited synagogues and schools in the area. In total, twenty-seven synagogues and some thirty schools were damaged or destroyed. The Porath Yosef, Hurva, and Tiferet Israel synagogues were destroyed. The famous Yohanan ben Zakkai Synagogue was devastated from within and survived only as a shell. The synagogue founded by the great biblical scholar Nachmanides in 1267 was also devastated. The loss to the Jewish heritage in Jerusalem was irreplaceable. Yet the destruction did not end there.

During Jordan's nineteen year rule of eastern Jerusalem, the hallowed Jewish cemetery on the Mount of Olives suffered a similar fate. As Gabriel Padon points out, "Graves had been ripped open and bones scattered; thousands of tombstones had been smashed or removed by the Jordanian Army to build fortifications, footpaths, army camps, and latrines. The Arab Jerusalem Municipality had granted concessions to merchants who destroyed graves and sold the gravestones to building contractors."[35] It is said that the original foundation stones of the Seven Arches Hotel (formerly the "Intercontinental") that stands on the Mount of Olives today, includes pieces taken from the Jewish cemetery.

The Jewish quarter was so thoroughly destroyed, according to news reporters, that it had the look of Stalingrad or Berlin in World War II. The quarter, emptied of its Jews, was turned over to squatters, mostly Arabs from the Hebron area, who used the remains of the synagogues as "stables, hen houses, rubbish dumps, and even latrines."[36] When Israeli soldiers regained the territory in June 1967 and entered the Yohanan ben Zakkai Synagogue complex, they found garbage piled to the ceiling.

The Israelis complained repeatedly to the United Nations about the Jordanian treatment of the Jewish quarter and the cemetery on the Mount of Olives. They claimed that Jordan's treatment violated the provisions of the truce agreement between the nations guaranteeing the safety of shrines and holy sites in their respective areas.[37]

---

[35] Gabriel Padon, "The Siege of Jerusalem," in Msgr. John M. Oesterreicher and Anne Sinai, eds., *Jerusalem* (New York: John Day, 1974), p. 101.

[36] Ibid.

[37] *Hashemite Kingdom of Jordan–Israel General Armistice Agreement*, April 3, 1949, 42 UNTS 304, in Lapidoth and Hirsch, *The Arab–Israel Conflict*, pp. 87–93.

There is little doubt that the Jordanians flagrantly violated the provision of the truce agreement that allowed for free access of peoples between the two parts of the city when they erected a wall of concrete and barbed wire to keep Jews from re-entering eastern Jerusalem and the Old City. Similarly, the Jordanians clearly violated truce provisions calling on both parties to ensure access to and preservation of the holy places. Jews were denied access to worship at the Western Wall and the synagogues. The barrier also prevented Muslims residing in Israel from visiting the Haram. So severe were the Jordanian restrictions against Jews gaining access to the Old City that visitors wishing to cross over from west Jerusalem (at the Mandelbaum Gate) had to produce a baptismal certificate. For their part, Jordanians cited desecration of Muslim graves by Israelis in the Mamilla Cemetery,[38] a few hundred meters west of the Old City. The Israelis heatedly denied this.

Shortly after Israel and Jordan signed the armistice agreement, Israel formally declared western Jerusalem its capital,[39] an action that did not meet with any more international approval than did Jordan's annexation of the West Bank (including eastern Jerusalem) in 1950.[40] The United States and other countries officially recognized the statehood of Israel, but they declined to acknowledge the legitimacy of Israel's incorporation of west Jerusalem as a national capital. The official position taken by Western leaders at the time was that the 1947 UN resolution affecting the internationalization of Jerusalem was still valid and that

---

[38] Discussing Israeli governance of Islamic holy sites in Israel between 1948 and 1967, Alisa Rubin Peled charges:

> While it was clear that all mosques fell under the umbrella of holy places, particularly the prominent ones whose treatment was closely monitored by the world, the designation of other types of sites, especially cemeteries, remained clouded in ambiguity. The (Israeli) Muslim Affairs Department took advantage of the ambiguous definition to neglect sites such as cemeteries, leading to shocking acts of desecration which provoked public scandals. The ministry went even further with bold moves to appropriate Muslim mosques for Jewish activities. . . . The Ministry of Foreign Affairs, ever conscious of the effect of these scandals on Israel's international reputation, fought to end the abuses, continually reminding the Muslim Affairs Department of the responsibility that went alongside its access to the tremendous financial resources of the *waqf* and the dire consequences of direct violations of the law. Between 1950 and 1955, the two Ministries thus became embroiled in an ever escalating conflict over the status and use of five Muslim sites: the Muslim cemeteries in Haifa and Mamilla (Jerusalem) and the mosques of al-Jazaar, Hassan Bek, and Sayidna Ali.

Alisa Rubin Peled, "The Crystallization of an Israeli Policy Towards Muslim and Christian Holy Places, 1948–1955," *Muslim World* 84, nos. 1–2 (January–April 1994), pp. 108–109.

[39] *Emergency Regulations (Land Requisition-Accommodation of State Institutions in Jerusalem) (Continuance in Force of Orders) Law*, in LSI 4 (1950), p. 106.

[40] Only two states, Britain and Pakistan, recognized Jordan's annexation of the West Bank, and only Britain recognized Jordanian control of Jerusalem—and even that was *de facto* recognition only.

both the Israeli and Jordanian actions to alter the status of Jerusalem were, from their point of view, illegitimate. The Vatican, in particular, stressed that the Christian holy places and surrounding Christian communities would be safeguarded only if the internationalization of Jerusalem, as proposed by the UN, was complete.

Both Israel and Jordan ignored outsiders' complaints about their actions and concentrated on governing their respective halves of Jerusalem. Since twenty-eight of the thirty holy places (as recognized by the UN) were in the Jordanian sector of Jerusalem, Jordan's responsibility for the care of these holy places was great. We have already discussed briefly Jordan's treatment of Jewish holy sites. What of the Christian sites?

For the most part Jordan, a Muslim state, adopted the Ottoman practice of viewing the various Christian communities as semi-autonomous *millets* (nations), led by their ethnarchs, who were free to administer their own communal affairs under the aegis of Islamic law.

There were some exceptions. In the case of the powerful Greek Orthodox Patriarchate of Jerusalem, custodian of many shrines and a major land owner, Jordan actively interceded (somewhat unsuccessfully) to break the hegemony that a minority of Greek bishops exercised over a church whose majority were Arab laity.[41] In 1958, Jordan passed legislation that governed the organization and management of property held by the Greek Orthodox Patriarchate of Jerusalem.[42] The government stipulated that Greek bishops had to be Jordanian citizens, speak and write Arabic, and that Arab bishops be ordained and appointed to the synod, the governing body of the Orthodox Church.[43] The Church accepted some of these stipulations and ignored others. The issue of the role of Arabs in the Greek Orthodox Patriarchate of Jerusalem became moot in 1967 when Israel conquered the Old City, and the Greek bishops, to their unspoken satisfaction, exchanged an Arab for a Jewish governing authority.[44]

Jordanian efforts to Arabize the Christian clergy met with more success among the Latin Patriarchate, where Arab priests were ordained and promoted to

---

[41] For a useful discussion of Jordan's policies affecting the Greek Orthodox and other Christians in Jerusalem, 1948–1967, see H. Eugene Bovis, *The Jerusalem Question 1917–1968* (Stanford, Calif.: Hoover Institution Press, 1971), pp. 95–99. See also Daphne Tsimhoni, *Christian Communities in Jerusalem and the West Bank Since 1948: An Historical, Social and Political Study* (Westport, Conn: Praeger, 1988), pp. 1–9, 36–46.

[42] *Law of the Eastern Greek Orthodox Patriarchate*, Law No. 27, *Official Gazette of the Kingdom of Jordan*, June 1, 1958, pp. 556–564 (Arabic).

[43] Ibid., at Chapter 6, article 19.

[44] Eugene Bovis notes that amid ongoing inter-Christian disputes, "One of the outstanding achievements during the Jordanian period was the agreement reached on June 27, 1961, by the Orthodox, Latins, and Armenians, with Jordanian government assistance, to carry out the necessary repairs to the Church of the Holy Sepulcher." H. Eugene Bovis, *The Jerusalem Question*, p. 96. No repairs actually took place while Jerusalem was under Jordanian rule.

the rank of bishop. These efforts coincided with Vatican II's emphasis on increasing indigenous local hierarchies. The result was the appointment of the first Arab Latin patriarch of Jerusalem and the virtually complete Arabization of the Anglican clergy of Jerusalem, including its presiding archbishop.

One problem for the Christian institutions was the Jordanian restrictions on the purchase of property, including property surrounding the holy places. The Jordanians in 1953 passed legislation prohibiting Christian charitable and religious institutions (local or foreign) from purchasing property in the vicinity of the holy places without express approval of the Jordanian Council of Ministers.[45] Local religious institutions were allowed to purchase property for religious purposes, whereas foreign religious institutions required a government license.[46] After considerable controversy, the law was amended to allow all religious institutions to purchase land freely for their own use but the prohibition against buying property in the area of the holy places remained intact.[47]

Jordan's conquest of the West Bank, the Old City, and eastern Jerusalem placed Jordan's King Abdullah as close as possible to his dream of leading the Arab "nation." Islam's third holiest city, the Mosque of al-Aqsa, and the Dome of the Rock shrine were all under Abdullah's protection. Yet, although Abdullah styled himself a protector of the holy sites, he did little to promote the religious importance of Jerusalem to Muslims. A supporter of the King was appointed both *mufti* (the government's religious leader) and president of the SMC. The position was made accountable to the chief *qadi* (religious judge) in Amman. Indeed, in 1951, the Council was abolished and a new body even more closely controlled by the king was created.[48] The treasury of the Palestine waqf was removed to Amman, and thereafter Muslim religious officials complained that little money found its way back to Jerusalem for upkeep of the mosques. The shari'a court in Jerusalem was integrated into Jordan's existing system and all Muslim judges were appointed from Amman. To Muslim Jerusalemites it was especially insulting that "Friday prayers were broadcast from the Great Husseini Mosque in

---

[45] *Law of Maintaining Properties by Religious Personalities*, Law No. 61, *Official Gazette of the Kingdom of Jordan,* April 16, 1953, Art. 7 (Arabic). The law states that "any charitable organization or religious institution or company, or any institution, Jordanian or foreign, does not have the right to attain, own or manage any real estate adjacent to religious holy sites unless a decision has been rendered by the Council of Ministers."

[46] Ibid., Articles 4 and 5.

[47] *Law of Maintaining Properties by Religious Personalities, amended on January 17, 1954.* In 1965, the law was further amended (Law No. 4, *Official Gazette of the Kingdom of Jordan,* January 18, 1965; Arabic). Daphne Tshimoni also points out that the amendment effectively precluded Christian religious institutions (foreign or domestic) from acquiring property near the holy places whether by deed or gift. Purchase of property in the Jerusalem District required special Cabinet approval; see *Christian Communities in Jerusalem and the West Bank since 1948*, p. 3.

[48] Michael Dumper, *The Politics of Jerusalem*, p. 167. See also Uri M. Kupferschmidt, *The Supreme Muslim Council, Islam under the British Mandate for Palestine*, pp. 257–258.

Amman instead of from the world's third most holy mosque [al-Aqsa] in Jerusalem."[49]

[49] Abu Shilbaya, "No Peace Without a Free Palestinian State" (Arabic), cited in Yehoshafat Harkabi, "The Palestinians in the Fifties and their Awakening as Reflected in Their Literature," in Moshe Ma'oz, ed. , *Palestinian Arab Politics* (Jerusalem: Jerusalem Academic Press, 1975), p. 78.

III

Israel's Unification of Jerusalem Since 1967

As a consequence of the third Arab–Israeli War of June 1967, Israel gained control of the Golan Heights, Sinai Peninsula, Gaza Strip, West Bank, and eastern Jerusalem, including the Old City. Israel moved swiftly to capitalize on this "miracle." One of the first acts of the Jewish government was to tear down the wall that had divided Arab-populated eastern Jerusalem and the Old City from the Jewish New City.

THE LEGAL POSITION

On June 27, 1967, the Knesset passed two laws that had the effect of expanding the boundaries of the Jerusalem Municipality.[1] The very next day the Knesset ordered "the application of Israeli law, jurisdiction, and administration" in eastern Jerusalem.[2] Jerusalem mayor Teddy Kollek and government officials spoke of the "unification" of Jerusalem; foreign critics spoke of annexation and questioned the legitimacy of Israel's policy. Israelis responded by arguing that eastern Jerusalem and the Old City were not annexed, but rather that the laws of Israel were extended to eastern Jerusalem and the Old City.[3]

The international law issues raised in this essay center on questions of sovereignty and responsibility toward the holy places. The sovereignty question

---

[1] *Law and Administration Ordinance (Amendment No. 11) Law, 27 June 1967*, in Ruth Lapidoth and Moshe Hirsch, eds., *The Arab–Israel Conflict and its Resolution: Selected Documents* (Boston: Martinus Nijhoff Publishers, 1991), p. 129. These allowed the government to extend Israeli "law jurisdiction and administration to any part of Mandatory Palestine by government order." *The Municipalities Ordinance (Amendment No. 6),* in LSI 21, (June 27, 1967), p. 75 (in Lapidoth and Hirsch, *The Arab–Israel Conflict*, p. 130) enabled the interior minister to enlarge the area of any municipality to include such areas.

[2] As a legal matter, it is worth noting that the Knesset never actually used the term annexation in 1967. Nor did it do so in 1980 with passage of the Basic Law of Jerusalem. *Basic Law: Jerusalem Capital of Israel,* in LSI 34 (July 30, 1980), p. 209. See Lapidoth and Hirsch, *The Arab–Israel Conflict*, p. 322. Nonetheless, it should be recognized that the Israeli Supreme Court in 1969 found that "united Jerusalem was an inseparable part of the state of Israel." *Hanzalis v. Greek Orthodox Patriarchate Religious Court*, translated in *International Law Reports*, p. 93, 94; see also *Iwad and Maches v. Military Court, Hebron District,* translated in *International Law Reports*, p. 63 (two Supreme Court judges hold that eastern Jerusalem had been annexed).

[3] Different assessments of the issues of annexation and sovereignty are made by Ruth Lapidoth, "Jerusalem—Some Jurisprudential Aspects," *Catholic University Law Review* 45 (1996), p. 661, and John Quigley, "Sovereignty in Jerusalem," *Catholic University Law Review* 45 (1996), p. 765.

turns, in part, on whether Jordan's claim of sovereignty over Jerusalem from 1948 to 1967 was accepted under international law. If this was the case, the Israelis could be described as "occupiers." Although one can occupy territory as a belligerent—that is to say, in self-defense until a peace treaty is signed— permanent occupation may well have questionable legal status.[4] Yet, many scholars have argued that Jordan's title to Jerusalem was itself flawed. Certainly Jordan had no historical claim, nor was its occupation accepted by other nations; indeed, only Pakistan recognized *de jure* Jordan's 1948 occupation of Jerusalem. Yet, whereas Jordan had no legitimate claim of "title" under international law, this does not imply that Palestine became, at the end of the Mandate, a *terra nullius*, a land owned by no one.[5] As Jordan had no legal claim, Israel had no need to 'return' conquered territory to Jordan or to the Palestinians, its arguable successor in title, as their title was no better than Israel's.[6] Although this argument has been made in regard to the entire West Bank, it has particular force as regards Jerusalem, because the UN General Assembly had voted specifically to make Jerusalem an internationalized city at the conclusion of the Mandate. Therefore, the entry of Glubb Pasha's Arab Legion on behalf of King Abdullah carried no international legitimacy, arguable or otherwise.[7]

---

[4] John Quigley, "Old Jerusalem: Whose to Govern?," *Denver Journal of International Law and Policy* 20 (1991), p. 145.

[5] Elihu Lauterpacht, *Jerusalem and the Holy Places*, pp. 41–42. See also Yehuda Z. Blum, "The Missing Reversioner: Reflections on the Status of Judea and Samaria," *Israel Law Review* 3 (1968), pp. 282–283. Such a conclusion, according to Blum, would lead to the "absurd result that a mandated territory would become . . . the helpless prey of external forces" (Ibid).

Although the doctrine of sovereignty in connection with former Mandate territories is complex, what is clear is that sovereignty rested somewhere. Lord McNair, in a separate opinion in *International Status of South West Africa*, concluded that modifications of status rested, in that case, "with the Union of South Africa acting with the consent of the United Nations." *International Status of South West Africa*, Advisory Opinion of July 11, 1950, ICJ Reports 1950, p. 143. Sovereignty over a Mandate territory, according to McNair, was in abeyance until such time as the inhabitants of the territory obtain recognition as an independent state. At that time, sovereignty would revive and vest in the new state. Ibid., p. 150. The Court's advisory opinion in *Western Sahara* bolstered this proposition by stating that Mandate territories inhabited by "peoples having a social and political organization were not regarded as *terra nullius*." *Western Sahara* (Request for Advisory Opinion), Order of May 22, 1975, ICJ Reports 1975, p. 39.

[6] One could argue that the question of sovereignty in Jerusalem has yet to be decided. After the British abandoned the Mandate, the entire population of Jerusalem, Palestinian and Jewish, was never given the opportunity to make a free determination on its political future. Hence, Allan Gerson suggests that "Israel's legitimate stake in the West Bank is limited to belligerent or, at best, trustee occupation, until the advent of a peace treaty establishing final recognized borders." Allan Gerson, *Israel, the West Bank and International Law* (London: Frank Cass, 1978), pp. 204–216.

[7] Although the validity of the Partition Resolution may be questioned, what remains clear is that sovereignty may not be claimed, nor is it transferred by occupation. This argument is more fully developed in Yehuda Blum, "The Missing Reversioner," pp. 283–89; see also Stephen M. Schwebel, "What Weight to Conquest?" *American Journal of International Law* 64 (1970), pp. 344, 346.

Notwithstanding overwhelming evidence to the contrary, some commentators, most forcefully John Quigley, have argued that both the 1948 and 1967 wars were wars of conquest on Israel's part.[8] International law strongly disfavors the acquisition of territory by conquest.[9] Thus, in discussing the 1967 war, Quigley argues that "[regarding] the eastern sector, it was indicated that Israel acted aggressively."[10] Whether it is the case that the Israeli Air Force struck first on June 5, 1967,[11] Quigley ignores completely that armed conflict, as that term is practically understood, already existed. As Timothy L.H. McCormack incisively suggests, "although the shooting had not actually commenced in earnest, preparations for the attack against Israel had reached the stage at which it could be argued that the attack had begun to occur and was instant and overwhelming." [12] Even if one does not accept this history, Quigley further ignores the accepted international law doctrine of "anticipatory self-defense."[13] And, as regards Jerusalem, it is clear that, Israel repeatedly requested King Hussein *not* to enter the war as a belligerent and that Israel attacked Jordanian positions in eastern Jerusalem only *after* the Jordanians repeatedly shelled Israeli-held western Jerusalem and occupied Government House.[14]

The gravamen of Quigley's legal position on Jerusalem is that Palestinians have sovereignty over all Jerusalem because they were the majority in Palestine in 1948. He never explains why that date serves as the historical cut-off. Nor

---

[8] Academic positions regarding whether the 1967 war was one of self-defense on the part of Israel are arrayed pro and con in Ruth Lapidoth's article, "Jerusalem and the Peace Process," *Israel Law Review* 28 (1994), pp. 402, 407, at note 21. A view that Israel was the aggressor in 1948 can be found in John Quigley, "Sovereignty in Jerusalem," p. 779.

[9] See generally Sharon Korman, *The Right of Conquest* (Oxford: Oxford University Press, 1996).

[10] John Quigley, "Sovereignty in Jerusalem," p. 779.

[11] As Prof. Amos Shapira points out, the issue of classification is as much a legal as a factual question, suggesting that "[e]ven if the United Nations record on this matter falls short of establishing an affirmative finding decisively upholding the lawfulness of Israel's action, at the very least, it provides solid support for Israel's claims to have acted in legitimate exercise of its right of self-defense." Amos Shapira, "The June 1967 War and the Right of Self-Defense," *Israel Law Review* 6 (1971), p. 80.

[12] Timothy L. H. McCormack, *Self-Defense In International Law: The Israeli Raid on the Iraqi Nuclear Reactor* (New York: St. Martin's Press, 1996), p. 273. McCormack does not classify Israel's actions in 1967 as anticipatory self-defense but rather as actual self-defense.

[13] The classic statement is in Philip C. Jessup, *A Modern Law of Nations* (New York: Archon Books, 1968), p. 163–166 (noting that the right of self-defense under customary international law included anticipatory actions against imminent threats). Anticipatory self-defense is further explicated in D. W. Bowett, *Self-Defence in International Law* (Manchester, England: Manchester University Press, 1958), pp. 185–192; Allen Gerson, *Israel, the West Bank and International Law*, pp. 15–18.

[14] Surprisingly, there is no definitive history of the June 1967 War. Nonetheless, in *A History of the Israeli Army: 1874 to the Present* (New York: Macmillan, 1985), pp. 131–32, 138–139, Ze'ev Schiff makes clear that Israel never expected to attack Jordan and never expected to take the Old City.

does he explain why one date is any more normative than another—particularly as Quigley chooses time lines that ignore 3,000 years of Jewish contact with the land of Israel.

In any event, whether or not Quigley's position is correct as regards the West Bank, it is difficult to see how he can even apply his own argument to Jerusalem, as the Jews were an undoubted majority in the city since the 1870 Ottoman census.[15] Further, Quigley fails to explain why the unit for classification is the whole of Palestine and not a part.[16]

Another arrow in Quigley's quiver is the UN General Assembly Partition Resolution of 1947. He now wishes to bind Israel to that resolution even though the Arabs rejected it at the time and many appear to reject it now. Quigley remains far out on a limb in claiming that the partition resolution has any legal effect in international law, as the consensus among international lawyers is that General Assembly resolutions are recommendations only.[17] Although some

---

[15] The general consensus of historians is that Jews first outnumbered Arabs in Jerusalem in the 1870s. See Yehoshua Ben-Arieh, *Jerusalem in the 19th Century: The Old City* (New York: St. Martin's Press, 1984), p. 276–279. While agreeing that "all available estimates do indicate a growing Jewish population in the Jerusalem region" during the late nineteenth century, Michael Dumper, in *The Politics of Jerusalem*, alleges that "discrepancies between sources and methods of enumeration make comparison and evaluation difficult during this period"; see p. 59–61. Without specifying years, Dumper concludes that "the Palestinian Arabs at this stage remained a clear majority although the exact proportions are disputed"; see p. 60.

Dumper fails to specify the "discrepancies" to which he alludes but does suggest that one should "balance" Ben-Arieh's figures with those of Justin McCarthy who, based on Ottoman census data, finds a large Palestinian majority in the Jerusalem *sanjak,* or administrative district; see Dumper, p. 282, note 10, and Justin McCarthy, *The Population of Palestine* (New York: Columbia University Press, 1990), pp. 6–7. Yet, Dumper's conclusion is problematic. First, as Dumper himself recognizes, the Ottoman census "only counted Ottoman nationals" and most Jewish immigrants maintained their European citizenship because of the numerous advantages afforded by the various capitulation treaties agreed to between the Sultan and the European powers; see p. 282, note 4. And, second, the sanjak of Jerusalem included numerous Arab villages outside the city and stretched as far as Jaffa and Gaza. Indeed, McCarthy himself recognizes that "we must fall back on secondary sources" for cities like Jerusalem, and he praises Ben-Arieh's analysis; see p. 15.

As to Dumper's suggestion (on p. 60) that traditional Ottoman census figures undercount Muslims as they include men only, McCarthy himself both points out that "women began to be included in the 1870s" (see p. 3) and develops demographic techniques for adjusting for any undercounting of young children (p. xix).

[16] John Quigley, "Old Jerusalem: Whose to Govern?" p. 764. Even if, based on the principle of self-determination, one were to accept this classification technique, Quigley does not deal with the possibility of two states being established in a territory that previously constituted one, as occurred between India and Pakistan. And indeed there is no principle in international law that would proscribe it.

[17] See Christopher C. Joyner, "U.N. General Assembly Resolutions and International Law: Rethinking the Contemporary Dynamics of Norm-Creation," *California Western International Law Journal* 11 (1981), pp. 452–453; see also Samuel A. Bleicher, "The Legal Significance of Re-Citation of General Assembly Resolutions," *American Journal of International Law* 63 (1969), pp.

scholars have suggested that certain UN resolutions, like the Universal Declaration of Human Rights, may have binding effect because they are evidence of or otherwise codify customary international law,[18] none of these special cases apply to a nonbinding General Assembly resolution.[19]

This discussion does not focus on the international law questions concerning the holy places. Here the issues turn on questions of protecting the character of the holy sites. Several international conventions and bilateral agreements impose obligations on Israel to undertake conduct that protects the holy places. These include the 1954 Hague Convention for the Protection of World Cultural and Natural Heritage,[20] designed to protect cultural property during conflict.[21]

Israel, notably, is not a member of an important follow-on to the Hague Convention, the 1972 United Nations Educational, Scientific, and Cultural Organization (UNESCO) Convention for the Protection of World Cultural and Natural Heritage.[22] This may be because of the treatment it suffered by UNESCO after the 1967 war. UNESCO, invoking the Hague Convention for the only time in its forty-year history, sent two commissioners to the area to examine damage to cultural property because of Israeli excavations around the Temple Mount and other areas. As part of this effort, both UNESCO and the Security Council asked

---

452–478.

[18] See, for example, Oscar Schacter, "International Law in Theory and Reality," *Receuil de Cours* 178 (1982-V), pp. 111–121.

[19] The distinction is between binding UN resolutions, which contribute to the emergence of customary rules originating in practice, and nonbinding resolutions, which neither constitute acts of conduct nor offer any conclusive evidence of any practice. Karol Wolfke, *Custom in Present International Law* (Boston: Martinus Nijhoff, 1993), pp. 83–84.

Even if one derives existence of a customary norm from both evidence of repeated practice (usage) and *opinio juris*, that is not the case here. Ibid., pp. 40–53. See also Anthony A. D'Amato, *The Concept of Custom in International Law* (Ithaca: Cornell University Press, 1971), p. 50.

[20] The 1954 *Hague Convention for the Protection of World Cultural and Natural Heritage* actually comprises four instruments: 1) Final Act of the Conference, May 14, 1954, 249 UNTS 215; 2) The Convention for the Protection of Cultural Property in the Event of Armed Conflict, May 14, 1954, 249 UNTS 240, with Regulations for the Execution of the Convention for the Protection of Cultural Property in the Event of Armed Conflict, May 14, 1954, 249 UNTS 270; 3) Protocol for Protection of Cultural Property in the Event of Armed Conflict, May 14, 1954, 249 UNTS 358; and, 4) Resolutions Adopted by the Conference, May 14, 1954, 249 UNTS 236.

[21] Article 1(a) of the Hague Convention defines "cultural property" broadly to include both religious and secular property.

[22] The Convention for the Protection of World Cultural and Natural Heritage, Doc. no. 17 C/106, November 15, 1972, in *International Law Materials* 11 (1973), p. 1358, requires party members to take steps to identify, preserve, protect, and conserve cultural and natural resources. See generally, James A. R. Nafzinger, "UNESCO-Centered Management of International Conflict Over Cultural Property," *Hastings Law Journal* 27 (1976), pp. 1051, 1058–1059; and Karen J. Detling, "Eternal Silence: The Destruction of Cultural Property in Yugoslavia," *Maryland Journal of International Law and Trade* 17 (1993), p. 41, notes 110–125.

Israel to halt such excavations.[23] Most independent observers viewed these complaints to be no more than foils to invoke yet another UN condemnation of Israel. Few have accepted the allegations that Israeli archaeological excavations in fact damaged Muslim holy sites.[24]

Issues of pilgrimage and access to the holy places are relevant as well. Although Israel has never recognized pilgrimage as a legal right, the Fundamental Agreement between the Holy See and Israel[25] states that both the Holy See and Israel "recognize that both have an interest in favoring Christian pilgrimages to the Holy Land."[26] The Agreement provides for consultation and cooperation between the proper agencies of the Church and the State when these pilgrimages occur. Further, §2 expresses the hope that "such pilgrimages will provide an occasion for better understanding between the pilgrims and the people and religions in Israel."[27]

The pilgrimage issue had previously raised concerns regarding the trade-off used by Israeli authorities when faced with competing claims of religious freedom and government regulation. Tour guides are extensively regulated in Israel both as to price and standards. Guides must pass comprehensive exams about the history and geography of the Holy Land. For their part the Catholic Church uses priests and religious figures as pilgrimage guides. After Israeli authorities in the late 1970s required that all tour groups be accompanied by licensed tour guides, the Church protested, claiming that applying the regulatory scheme to church groups interfered with its traditional rights of pilgrimage. Happily, wiser heads prevailed and the matter was laid to rest in July 1981 when Israeli officials and the Catholic Church agreed that pilgrim groups, because of

---

[23] UNESCO went further. On November 20, 1974, UNESCO's General Conference adopted, by a vote of 59–33, a resolution condemning Israel for its excavations on the Temple Mount and directing the organization's Director General to withhold assistance from Israel. The following day, the General Conference rejected an Israeli initiative to be included in UNESCO's European regional group. Gordon Lang, "UNESCO and Israel," *Harvard International Law Journal* 16 (1975), p. 676.

[24] This point is underscored by Nafzinger and Lang, who even question the application of the Hague Convention to the dispute. See James A. R. Nafzinger, "UNESCO-Centered Management of International Conflict Over Cultural Property," pp. 1057–1059, and Gordon Lang, "UNESCO and Israel," p. 677.

[25] See the *Fundamental Agreement between the Holy See and State of Israel*, signed in Jerusalem, December 30, 1993, *International Legal Materials* 33 (1994), p. 153.

[26] Ibid., at Article 5, §1. This does not mean that the Fundamental Agreement creates any international obligations regarding the rights of pilgrimage. In contrast, some have proposed that the right of pilgrimage to the holy places be protected by international guarantee. Peter W. Mason, "Pilgrimage to Religious Shrines: An Essential Element in the Human Right to Freedom of Thought, Conscience, and Religion," *Case Western Reserve Journal of International Law* 25 (1993), p. 619.

[27] *Fundamental Agreement between the Holy See and the State of Israel*, p. 155.

their specific religious and spiritual needs, should be guided by religious officials under the guidance of the Church.[28]

ADMINISTERING JERUSALEM'S HOLY PLACES

Through passage of the Protection of Holy Places Law,[29] the Israeli government sought to assure Christians and Muslims that their monuments were safe under Jewish government. That law states,

> The holy places shall be protected from desecration and any other violation and from anything likely to violate the freedom of access of the members of the various religions to the places sacred to them or their feelings with regard to those places. Whoever does anything that is likely to violate the freedom of access of the members of the various religions to the places sacred to them or their feelings with regard to those places shall be liable to imprisonment for a term of five years. [30]

Indeed Israel defended its 1967 extension of jurisdiction as a measure undertaken (in part) to protect the holy places. In a 1967 letter to the UN Secretary General, Abba Eban argued that "the measures adopted relate to the integration of Jerusalem in the administrative and municipal spheres, and furnish the legal basis for the protection of the holy places of Jerusalem."[31]

Except for an aborted effort in the summer of 1967 to demand preclearance of sermons at the Haram, Israel's conduct regarding the holy places, while certainly not perfect, must be considered exemplary. Even before the now immortal handshake on September 13, 1993, Muslims from Saudi Arabia and Libya were allowed to undertake the pilgrimage to pray at al-Aqsa mosque in the Old City. And Israel reversed the earlier Jordanian law that forbade Christian denominations from acquiring land or homes in Jerusalem by purchase or gift.[32]

---

[28] The entire affair is discussed in a paper presented by Fr. Richard Mathes of the Pontifical Institute in Jerusalem—"Forerunner to the Vatican–Israel Accord: Issues of Pilgrimage"—at a conference on *The Fundamental Agreement between the Holy See And The State of Israel: A Third Anniversary Perspective,* at the Columbus School of Law, Catholic University of America, Washington, D.C., April 8, 1997.

[29] See *Protection of the Holy Places Law,* in LSI 21 (June 27, 1967), p. 76, sec. 1 (cited in Lapidoth and Hirsch, *The Arab-Israel Conflict,* p. 169), and reiterated in the *Basic Law: Jerusalem, Capital of Israel,* sec. 3 (cited in Lapidoth and Hirsch, *The Arab–Israel Conflict,* p. 324). For discussion of the *Protection of Holy Places Law,* see Walter Zander, *Israel and the Holy Places of Christendom* (New York: Praeger Publishers, 1971), pp. 102–110.

[30] See *Protection of the Holy Places Law,* p. 76, no. 2(b), in Lapidoth and Hirsch, *The Arab–Israel Conflict,* p. 169.

[31] *Measures Taken by Israel to Change the Status of the City of Jerusalem: Report of the Secretary General,* July 10, 1967, UN Doc. A/6753 at 3, in *International Legal Materials* 6 (1967), pp. 846, 848.

[32] The lifting of restrictions on the sale and leasing of Church property led, in subsequent years, to major transfers of property to Jewish control from the Armenian and Greek Orthodox Churches. Such property transfers would become a continuing source of grievances expressed by Palestinian

The authorities have generally allowed the waqf autonomy in its administration of the holy places. In July 1967, twenty two Muslim dignitaries founded a new *Hay'a al-Islamiyya* (Supreme Muslim Council) to protest the occupation and protect Muslim religious rights.[33] Indeed, for more than two decades—until 1993—the head of the Supreme Muslim Council in Jerusalem was in fact an employee of the Jordanian government. He served as the Jordanian-appointed chief *qadi* for eastern Jerusalem as well as chairman of the Muslim waqf for eastern Jerusalem and the West Bank. (And as such he reported to the Jordanian minister of waqfs.) A disinterested observer could well conclude that Israel has proffered more autonomy to the waqf, "under more trying circumstances, than did the British in the last decade of the Mandate."[34]

It was a different story with respect to the Christian holy places. Here the Ministry of Religious Affairs maintained effective contacts with Christian leaders and responded to their needs.[35] The ministry ordered police protection for the shrines and a general clean-up for the areas around the principal churches. It compensated several of the Christian communities for damage done to churches during the 1967 war, even when the damage was not directly due to Israeli fire.

From 1967 until 1973, Israel presided over the administration of the holy places without great criticism from within the country or from abroad. One exception was the Muslim charge that the Israeli government acted illegally and immorally in razing the Mugrabi quarter to make room for the Western Wall plaza. Muslims regarded the Mugrabi area, containing a collection of brick hovels, as waqf property.[36] Another exception was the damage done in 1969 to

---

Christians against their non-Arab church leaders. This history is detailed in Michael Dumper, *The Politics of Jerusalem*, pp. 185–192.

[33] The SMC numbered fifty-one members by 1992. Yitzhak Reiter, *Islamic Institutions in Jerusalem* (London: Kluwer Law International, 1997), p. 10.

[34] Ibid., pp. 9–10.

[35] At this time, Christian leaders communicate with Israeli officials through the Christian desk officers of the Ministry of Religious Affairs and the Ministry of Foreign Affairs because so many Christian institutions have parent bodies situated in foreign countries. On matters connected with Jerusalem, the mayor's special assistant for Christian affairs is available to deal with problems. For their part, Muslims interact with the Office of Muslim Affairs within the Ministry of Religious Affairs or with the Ministry of the Interior, or for matters pertaining to Jerusalem, they see the special adviser to the mayor on Arab affairs. All these officials meet together on a regular basis to discuss matters of mutual concern. If Muslim or Christian religious matters in Jerusalem influence the West Bank, a representative of the civil administration joins them. This mechanism has many flaws, not least of which is that the fracturing of authority between all these offices often makes decision making difficult.

Michael Dumper suggests that these arrangements became more difficult under recent Likud rule and since "the Likud showed less sensitivity to church concerns, [it] caused the gradual erosion of the cooperative and consultative arrangements that had previously been established"; see *The Politics of Jerusalem*, p. 194. Yet, Dumper fails to provide sources for this provocative assertion.

[36] For an analysis of the controversy surrounding the Mugrabi Quarter demolition, see Meron Benvenisti, *Jerusalem: The Torn City* (Minneapolis: University of Minnesota Press, 1976), pp.

the al-Aqsa mosque by an arson attack carried out by Dennis Michael Rohan, a Christian fundamentalist visitor from Australia. Muslims blamed Israel for the damage to the mosque, but a commission of inquiry later determined that Rohan was deranged, acted alone, and that considerable damage could have been avoided if the Muslim authorities supervising the mosque had acted with greater dispatch and competence.[37]

The relative calm that Israel enjoyed in carrying out a military occupation of more than a million Arabs in the West Bank and Gaza evaporated after the Yom Kippur War of October 1973. Whereas Israel was the clear victor, the Palestinians experienced a renewed nationalistic consciousness, which led in subsequent years to strikes, shutdowns, demonstrations, and bloody riots. This unrest exploded in 1987 with the *intifada*, the Palestinian "revolt" against Israeli occupation. Although the intifada was less strong in Jerusalem, it served to divide the city and to underscore the separation of the religious and ethnic groups.

305–309.
[37] Ibid., pp. 300–304.

IV

The Interests of the Christian Community

The members of the Christian community in Jerusalem have at least two concerns regarding the holy places in Jerusalem. First, they are concerned to have their "rights" in the holy places and the city in some way confirmed (or reconfirmed) in international law.[1] And second, they are concerned with ensuring rights of access,[2] freedom of religious activity, and freedom of pilgrimage to the holy places and the Holy City.

Christians face three practical problems that affect their approach to these issues. First, they are fractured and are as concerned that another church might secure advantages they do not have as they are that the general interests of the Christian community be considered.[3] They therefore insist on the Ottoman "status quo" at all times, even if doing so might hurt their individual interests. As an example, the different denominations that claim possessory interests in the Church of the Holy Sepulcher jealously guard every inch of "title," every presumption of customary privilege they can. Similarly, the Copts (an Egyptian Christian Church) and the Ethiopian Christians have disputed for centuries over the monastery of Deir al Sultan, east of the Church of the Holy Sepulcher. It was in the Copts' possession until Easter night 1970, when the Ethiopians entered the monastery and changed the locks while the Copts were at church. In protest, the Copts "camped out" in an encampment of huts by their old home. Efforts to remedy this reversal of fortune remain mired in the Israeli legal process.[4]

---

[1] The Vatican's position toward Jerusalem and the holy places has remained consistent since it abandoned its insistence on the city's internationalization. Its focus is to pursue an international statute or document that would both ensure the protection of the holy places and the historical and religious character of the city, and guarantee the civil and religious rights of the communities in Palestine. Silvio Ferrari and Francesco Margiotta Broglio, "The Vatican, the European Community, and the status of Jerusalem," in *Studi in Memoria di Mario Condorelli* 3 (Milan: Giuffrè Editore, 1988), pp. 580–587.

[2] "Access rights" includes practical, not merely formal, access.

[3] For historical background, see text above, pp. 5–6.

[4] In HCJ 109/70, *The Coptic Patriarchate v. The Minister of Police*, 25 (1) PD 225 (1971), the Copts secured an order of eviction. Enforcement was postponed to allow a government committee to make determinations as to substantive rights under the 1924 Order in Council. See the *Palestine (Holy Places) Order in Council* of 1924, in L. G. A. Cust, *The Status Quo in the Holy Places* (Jerusalem: Ariel Publishing House, 1980), pp. 65–66. The committee met once since 1971, but a second petition in 1977—based on grounds that the court was waiting for the government to act— failed. See HCJ 188/77, *The Coptic Patriarchate v. The Government of Israel*, 33 (1) PD 225

Even today, the different Christian communities remain at odds. It has taken more than thirty years to create a consensus among the different denominations present at the Church of the Holy Sepulcher as to how to proceed with vital building repairs.[5] A consensus was only reached among the denominations after Israeli officials, fearing a cave-in, threatened to make the repairs to the ceiling themselves. A dispute over the painting of the dome of the rotunda took more than twelve years to resolve.[6]

Indeed, the Greek Orthodox have often indicated that maintenance of Israeli control of Christian holy places was preferable to revision of the Ottoman status quo.[7] In any revision, they fear, they would lose out to the larger and more powerful Roman Catholic Church.[8] In speaking of the holy places, Patriarch Diodoros I underscored that "the Vatican does not represent us."[9] In late 1995, he issued a call for a legally binding agreement with Israel that would not compromise the existing status quo.[10] (Similar intramural tension might be expected among Muslim interests if Israel were to ask them to "govern" the Muslim holy places.)

The second practical problem the Christian Churches face is that most of the lay Christian in the Jerusalem area are Palestinians, who do not wish (out of either solidarity or fear) to isolate themselves from general Palestinian concerns.

(1979). At different times both the Egyptian and Ethiopian governments have intervened on behalf of their "charges." See generally, Walter Zander, "Jurisdiction and Holiness: Reflections on the Coptic–Ethiopian Case," *Israel Law Review* 17 (1982), p. 245.

[5] See Lisa Pevtzow, "Holy Squabbles," *Jerusalem Post*, April 1, 1994, p. 6, for a description of the territorial battles among the six religious denominations housed in the church.

[6] Mary Curtius, "Holy Sepulcher Church Paint Job an Act of Faiths," *Los Angeles Times*, April 15, 1995, p. 1. See also Michael Krikorian, "Religion: A Simple Cross Ends Decades of Division," *Los Angeles Times*, December 30, 1995, p. 4.

Although George Doty, a Roman Catholic investment banker from Rye, New York, provided the funding, he stressed that all the work had taken place within the framework of the "status quo." Haim Shapiro, "Holy Sepulcher cupola unveiled after 68 years under wraps," *Jerusalem Post*, January 3, 1997, p. 20. Only after seeking the assistance of the Pontifical Mission for Palestine, a social services organization, was Doty able to secure the agreement of all the religious "stakeholders" to begin the restoration. Graziano Motta, "Jerusalem Basilica's dome is restored," *L'Osservatore Romano*, weekly edition, February 8–19, 1997, p. 8.

[7] Haim Shapiro, "Greek Orthodox: Consult Us on Status of Holy Places," *Jerusalem Post*, July 20, 1994, p. 124.

[8] On November 14, 1994, the Greek Orthodox Church, together with eleven other Churches' leaders, signed a memorandum—"The Significance of Jerusalem for Christians"—calling for the maintenance of the status quo as regards the Christian holy places (on file with author). The Catholic Church had already adopted that position the 1993 accord with Israel. See *Fundamental Agreement between the Holy See and the State of Israel*, signed in Jerusalem, December 30, 1993, as reprinted in *International Legal Materials* 33 (1994), at Art. 4, sec. 1.

[9] Haim Shapiro, "Patriarch Wants Agreement Between non-Catholic Church and Israel," *Jerusalem Post*, December 29, 1995, p. 1.

[10] Ibid.

Most of their clergy (including the senior clergy), however, are from European countries, and their interests thus may not mesh with those of the Palestinian laity.[11]

And, third, there is a real concern with maintaining a sufficient Christian community in Jerusalem to serve as "witness" to Christian needs and concerns. This demographic problem may not be the fault of any specific party, but it is real. Since 1948, the Christian community of Jerusalem has dropped in size from 30,000 to between 10,000 and 12,000. Bethlehem, where Church tradition places Jesus' birth, no longer has a Christian majority.[12] Rev. Peter Vasko, a Franciscan priest and president of the Holy Land Foundation, has lamented, "If we don't do something now, within sixty to seventy years there will be no Christian churches in the Holy Land. . . . Christian holy sites will be empty monuments."[13]

The Christian community should not assume that they need only be concerned with their relations with the Israeli government. The Palestinian Ministry of Religion recently appointed Ibrahim Kandallaf, a Greek Orthodox resident of eastern Jerusalem, to be adviser on Christian affairs. Although Kandallaf's authority extends only to areas within the control of the Palestinian Authority (PA) where there are few Christian holy sites, he in fact operates *de facto* in Jerusalem as a whole, joining Israeli officials on the dais at Christian events in eastern Jerusalem.[14] Moreover, the Christian community cannot be certain that his authority will not be enlarged. Indeed, it is reported that the so-called Abu Mazen–Beilin "non-paper" on final status issues, including Jerusalem, called for the Church of the Holy Sepulcher to be placed under extraterritorial Palestinian jurisdiction.[15] The Christian communities may have no

---

[11] One exception is the Latin patriarch, His Excellency Michel Sabbah, the first Palestinian Christian to hold that office. His views are laid out in "The Church of Jerusalem: Living with Conflict, Working for Peace," *Commonweal* 123, no. 1 (January 12, 1996), p. 14.

[12] It is unclear what, if anything, can be done to resolve this problem. It may be necessary for the municipality to consider providing housing assistance for Christians in the Old City—where most of them live—in the same way that the government of Israel provides incentives for building new areas for Jewish settlement. Although this may cause problems for Israel, which has historically not distinguished between Palestinian Christians and Muslims, some focus on this issue may be needed to preserve Christian life in the Holy Land.

[13] Cited in David Gibson, "Holy Land's Christians in Need of Miracle," *The Record* (Bergen City, N.J.), December 26, 1996, p. A1.

[14] Bill Hutman, "Olmert: PA official liasing with churches," *Jerusalem Post*, November 28, 1996, p. 2.

[15] The Abu Mazen–Beilin non-paper was concluded and initialed in November 1996 but was never accepted by either Arafat or then–Prime Minister Simon Peres. See Ze'ev Schiff, "Beilin and Abu Mazen Drafted a Document on Final Status; Agreed to Establish a Palestinian State," *Ha'aretz*, February 22, 1996, p. 1 (Hebrew); Rachel Ingber, "The Past, Present and Future of the Oslo Process: View from the Labor Party," Washington Institute for Near East Policy, *Peace Watch*, no. 112 (December 11, 1996) (summarizing speech of Yossi Beilin); David Makovsky, "Time for Beilin to disclose agreement in full," *Jerusalem Post*, February 25, 1996, p. 2.

choice but to also negotiate with the Palestinians as well as with the Israelis. Recently, Israeli officials suggested that the Muslim authorities might be planning to tear down a Christian holy site, Jesus' cradle, which is located on the Temple Mount, but the Palestinians heatedly denied it.[16] And in July 1997, the PA evicted a "White Russian" contingent from a church in Hebron, which the PA controls under the Oslo Agreement, and presented the church building to representatives of the Russian patriarch in Moscow.[17]

CATHOLIC VIEWS

With the entry into Jerusalem of the British army under Lord Edmund Allenby in 1917, the Holy See sought a seat at the table deciding Jerusalem's fate. Its goal was control of Palestine by a Western power—preferably Catholic. This desire was not mitigated by World War II.[18] Both at the time of the 1947 partition plan and afterwards, the Vatican supported an international city.[19] Yet, after the June 1967 War, the Vatican began to move away from its insistence on the creation of a *corpus separatum,* or separate legal jurisdiction, and toward support for international guarantees to safeguard the uniqueness of the city.[20]

In December 1993, the Vatican signed an accord with Israel that led to mutual recognition and the exchange of ambassadors.[21] The bilateral accord deals

---

[16] Karin Laub, "Foreign Minister asks Police to Monitor Christian Holy Site," *AP Worldstream*, December 3, 1996.

[17] See Serge Schmemann, "Arafat Enters Into a New Fray Over a Russian Church," *New York Times,* July 11, 1997, p. A3.

[18] By World War II, the Vatican knew that Catholic control over Palestine "was unattainable, and in the actual circumstances it preferred tre [sic] Arabs to the Jews." John Victor Perowne, British plenipotentiary minister to the Holy See, cited in Ferrari and Margiotta Broglio, "The Vatican, the European Community, and the status of Jerusalem," pp. 573–574. The comment was made during the summer of 1949.

[19] See the discussion of internationalization in the following articles by Silvio Ferrari: "The Religious Significance of Jerusalem in the Middle East Peace Process: Some Legal Implications," *Catholic University Law Review* 45 (1996), p. 733; "The Struggle for Jerusalem," *European Journal of International Affairs* 11 (1991), pp. 22–39; and "The Vatican, Israel, and the Jerusalem Question (1943–1984)," *Middle East Journal* 39, no. 2 (Spring 1985), pp. 316–331. See also Andrej Kreutz, *Vatican Policy in the Palestinian–Israeli Conflict* (New York: Greenwood Press, 1990), pp. 93–94.

[20] Ferrari and Margiotta Broglio, "The Vatican, the European Community, and the status of Jerusalem," p. 583.

[21] See the *Fundamental Agreement between the Holy See and State of Israel*, signed in Jerusalem, December 30, 1993, *International Legal Materials* 33 (1994), p. 153. See also "Amman, Vatican Call For Shared Custody of Religious Sites," *Jerusalem Post,* July 10, 1994, p. 2, for a discussion of remarks by Vatican foreign minister Jean-Lois Tauran; Chaim Bermant, "Rome Turns Toward Jerusalem," *Independent* (London), December 21, 1993, p. 14, for a description of the history of the conflict between Jews and the Vatican; and Peter Hebblethwaite, "Vatican Recognition of Israel Changes History," *National Catholic Reporter*, January 7, 1994, p. 10, for an examination of the

with a variety of issues, such as political recognition, pilgrimage, religious freedom, and access to the holy places. As the Accord states, "the State of Israel affirms its continuing commitment to maintain and respect the 'status quo' in the Christian holy places to which it applies and the respective rights of the Christian communities thereunder."[22]

The Catholic Church still has outstanding issues with Israel. An agreement on the legal personality of the Catholic Church in Israel was approved on September 7, 1997 by the government of Israel.[23] An agreement on tax exemption remains to be negotiated. These issues revolve around the tax privileges of clergy and tax exemption for religious property, and they draw on an understanding Israel reached in 1948 with France (as interlocutor for the Catholic community).[24] The long delay in reaching closure on these negotiations has stalled the flowering of Vatican–Israeli relations.

The Vatican has also moved toward establishing official links with the Palestinian Liberation Organization (PLO). In an effort to promote the peace process, following several months of negotiations, in October 1994 the Vatican

---

relations between Israel and the Vatican that notes the Catholic Church's concern over Jerusalem's holy places).

[22] See the *Fundamental Agreement between the Holy See and State of Israel*, at Art. 4, §1, p. 155. As Meron Benvenisti points out, Israel in 1967 never affirmed the status quo in the Christian holy places in such terms, because the status quo in fact inhibited Jewish presence at Muslim holy places such as the Temple Mount. Meron Benvenisti, *City of Stone: The Hidden History of Jerusalem*, pp. 99–100. *The Protection of Holy Places Law*, June 27, 1967, did however affirm that "the holy places shall be protected from desecration and any other violation and from anything likely to violate the freedom of access of the members of the different religions."

[23] *Legal Personality Agreement with the Holy See*, November 11, 1997, Consulate General of Israel, New York. The purpose of the agreement was to normalize the status and legal personality of the Catholic Church and its institutions in Israel. The agreement determined that the Catholic Church and many of its institutions would be accorded legal status under Israeli law. The institutions would be included in an official state registry and their interaction with non-Church bodies in Israel will be subject to Israeli law—including litigation in Israeli courts. Church institutions would, however, maintain full internal autonomy in the administration of its institutions and assets in Israel. Adjudication of these matters would be left to the Church in accordance with Canon law. By entering into the agreement, Israel committed itself "not only to the *de jure* confirmation of those rights pertaining to the Catholic Church's educational and philanthropic institutions, but also to enshrine the authoritative structure of the Church's hierarchy and religious orders in Israeli law." David Rosen, "New Agreement between Vatican and Israel yet another stop on the journey of reconciliation," *Irish Times*, November 18, 1997, p. 14.

[24] The so-called "secret" agreement between France and Israel was actually an exchange of letters between the representative of the Jewish Agency in Paris and the Director General of the French Foreign Ministry. The Catholic Church claims that the exchange constituted an agreement by Israel to continue the privileges and exemptions obtained during the British Mandate and Ottoman period. Israeli authorities, however, argue that it was merely an agreement to conduct negotiations over whether the arrangements should continue to have effect. France and Israel have been debating the issue for more than 40 years. "Comments on the Fundamental Agreement between the Holy See and the State of Israel," an interview with Eitan Margalit, *Justice*, no. 2 (June 1994), p. 25.

and the PLO announced the establishment of official links. The PLO opened an office at the Vatican and the papal nuncio in Tunis became responsible for the Vatican's contacts with PLO leaders. In a joint statement issued by the Vatican, the parties announced that the official links would "open channels for communication" to "jointly . . . search for peace and justice . . . in the Middle East" with a view toward "preserving the religious and cultural values which mark the peoples of the region, and which properly belong to the Holy Land and especially to the Holy City of Jerusalem."[25]

Having recognized the State of Israel and the PLO, the Vatican now hopes to have a "seat at the table" when final status issues are discussed.[26] The Vatican has asserted its position in the Jerusalem question as not only a matter of right, but "a right which it exercises to express moral judgment on the situation."[27] However described, this "right" does not extend to such "technical aspects" as the territorial boundaries of the city or its form of governance.[28] Rather, the Vatican's concerns center on three objectives.

First, the Vatican has consistently promoted the adoption of an "internationally guaranteed special statute."[29] The goals of such a statute would be 1) to safeguard the global character of Jerusalem as a sacred heritage common to the three monotheistic religions; 2) to preserve religious freedom in all aspects; 3) to protect the status quo; 4) to assure permanence and the development of religious, educational, and social activities proper to each community; 5) to ensure equality of treatment to all three religions; and 6) to establish an

---

[25] "PLO, Vatican establish links, but not full diplomatic recognition," *Deutsche Presse-Agentur,* October 25, 1994. See also "Joint Communication between the Holy See and the Palestinian Liberation Organization," *Bollettino Sala Stampa Della Santa Sede,* October 25, 1994 (on file with author) (Italian). The pope most recently received a delegation of the Palestinian Authority led by Emil M. Jorjovi, a member of the PLO Executive Committee and the Palestinian Legislative Council, in September, 1997. "Pope Meets Members of Palestinian Authority," *Vatican Information Service,* September 22, 1997.

[26] The Vatican Secretary of State for Foreign Affairs, Archbishop Jean-Louis Tauran, has pointed out that "[t]he religious aspect of Jerusalem must be discussed in a multilateral forum and we want to be involved in it." "Vatican Official: Nobody Can Claim Exclusive Rights to Holy Places," *Jerusalem Post,* December 19, 1995, p. 1.

[27] "Vatican Note: Jerusalem, Considerations of the Secretariat of State," *Origins: Catholic News Service Documentary Service* 26, no. 16 (October 3, 1996), p. 250. Indeed, this right is contained in Article 11 of the *Fundamental Agreement between the Holy See and the State of Israel,* which provides that the Holy See maintains the right, in every case, to exercise its moral and spiritual teaching office.

[28] Ibid., p. 253. The Holy See "is not concerned with the question of how many square meters or kilometers constitute the disputed territory." Still, it is important to underscore its view that "a political solution will not be valid unless it takes into account in a profound and just manner the religious needs present in the city."

[29] "Civilta Cattolica: The Future of Jerusalem," excerpted in *Origins: Catholic News Service Documentary Service* 26, no. 16 (October 3, 1996), p. 256.

"appropriate juridical safeguard" that does not reflect the will of only one of the interested parties involved.[30]

As a matter of principle, then, the Vatican adheres to the view that the issues surrounding Jerusalem are of concern to more than the two parties involved and that there is a unique international interest in what happens to the Holy City.[31] As one authoritative Vatican source has noted, "When it comes to Jerusalem, the voice of others [besides Israelis and Palestinians], the presence of additional subjects legitimized by international law, and the appropriate contribution of religious and cultural institutions cannot be considered superfluous or unsuitable."[32]

One reflection of the Vatican's rejection of bipolarity was the controversial appeal to U.S. president Bill Clinton by Cardinal William Keeler, then president of the National Conference of Catholic Bishops, seeking a greater Christian voice in discussions over the future of Jerusalem.[33] The letter evoked considerable controversy in the Jewish community. At a meeting with Jewish leaders after the appeal appeared, Cardinal Keeler seemed to modify his position. Keeler issued a

---

[30] Edmond Farhat, ed., *Gerusalemme nei Documenti Pontifici* (Jerusalem in Pontifical Documents) (Vatican City: Libreria Editrice Vaticana, 1987) (Italian).

[31] This view has been consistently promoted by the Vatican. Pope Paul VI first called for "a special statute, whose observation would be guaranteed by an institution international in character." Robert C. Doty, "Pope Asks Peace without Victory; Offers Own Aid," *New York Times*, December 23, 1967, p. 1. One year later, on December 23, 1968, the Pope reaffirmed this position by calling for "an internationally generated regulation of the question of Jerusalem and the holy places." "Address of Pope Paul VI to the College of Cardinals," in *The Pope Speaks* 13 (Huntington, Ind.: Our Sunday Visitor, Inc., 1968), pp. 313–314. The notion of a special statute was reinforced by Pope John Paul II in a statement worded by the Permanent Observer to the Holy See to the UN on December 3, 1979, included in Edmond Farhat, ed., *Gerusalemme nei Documenti Pontifici*, pp. 214–216. Since that time, the Pope has supported the inclusion of other international players, first and most important, in the apostolic letter *Redemptionis Anno* (April 20, 1984), included in *The Pope Speaks* 29 (Huntington, Ind.: Our Sunday Visitor, Inc., 1984), pp. 219–222, in which he said "the entire human race, and especially the peoples and nations who have brothers in faith in Jerusalem—Christians, Jews, and Muslims—has reason to feel involved in this matter and to do everything possible to preserve the unique and sacred character of the city." The pope reemphasized this message most recently on January 13, 1996, during an address to the diplomatic corps, accredited to the Holy See and included in *Origins: Catholic News Service Documentary Service* 25, no. 31 (January 25, 1996), pp. 526–528.

[32] "Civilta Cattolica: The Future of Jerusalem," p. 254.

[33] The appeal, dated March 6, 1995, was entitled *Jerusalem: City of Peace*. The full text was printed in *Origins: Catholic News Service Documentary Service* 24, no. 40 (March 23, 1995), pp. 671–672. Seven Christian leaders signed the letter. Other signatories were leaders of the Episcopal Church, the Evangelical Lutheran Church in America, the American Friends Service Committee, and the Greek Orthodox Archdiocese of North and South America. Later signatories included the leadership of the World Methodist Council North America Section, Disciples of Christ, and the United Church of Christ.

clarification[34] underscoring that the appeal was intended as a plea "to preserve all options and possible solutions until the principals could address them."[35]

The Vatican's second concern is for the environmental and cultural character of the Jerusalem it cares about most—the Old City. It wants the surrounds of the holy places to reflect their august majesty and it needs a living community of the faithful to breathe life into what would otherwise be holy relics. More than anything, it is this demographic concern that keeps the Vatican from limiting its concerns to the holy places themselves.[36]

A recent *Civilta Cattolica* article suggested that some of these concerns might be met if the political parties immediately involved (i.e., the Israelis and Palestinians) were to "meet obligations of the kind involved in the 1972 UNESCO Convention on the Protection of World Cultural and Natural Heritage."[37] As articulated in UNESCO's 1976 Recommendation Concerning the Safeguarding and Contemporary Role of Historic Areas, "protection is to be given not only to the buildings, but to the whole spacial structure, the environment, and the human activities comprised within the area which is meant for protection."[38]

---

[34] The text of the clarification may be found in *Origins: Catholic News Service Documentary Service* 24, no. 40 (March 23, 1995), p. 672; see also Frank P. L. Sommerville, "Keeler, Jewish Leaders, and Jerusalem," *Baltimore Sun*, March 26, 1995, p. 1B.

[35] Michael James and Frank P. L. Sommerville, "Keeler Seeks to Calm U.S. Jewish Leaders," *Baltimore Sun*, March 14, 1995, p. 1A; see also, Frank P. L. Sommerville, "Keeler's Clarifying Letter Mollifies Jewish Leaders," *Baltimore Sun*, March 15, 1995, p. 1B.

Nonetheless, Cardinal Keeler was quite careful to reaffirm the substance of the March 6 letter, saying that "what occasioned the Christian letter [i.e., the 6 March letter] remains the substance of the issue . . ." See *Origins: Catholic News Service Documentary Service,* p. 572, note 114. See Haim Shapiro, "Bernadin: Keeler Statement Doesn't Speak for U.S. Bishops," *Jerusalem Post*, April 19, 1995, p. 6, in which Cardinal Joseph Bernadin underscores that the substance of the Christian leaders' statement is "consistent with existing Catholic policy."

Jewish leaders had feared that the letter may have differed from the 1989 statement by the U.S. Bishops, "Toward Peace in the Middle East: Perspective, Principles and Hopes," with which Jewish leaders felt comfortable. See *Origins: Catholic News Service Documentary Service* 19, no. 25 (November 23, 1989), pp. 410–411, for a discussion of Jerusalem. Yet, as Cardinal Keeler pointed out in his March 15 clarification, the 1995 statements cannot be appreciated outside the context of the 1989 statement.

[36] This concern for the indigenous population is not new. By late 1948 the Vatican wanted to underscore the extent to which "believers preempted buildings in the Vatican's priorities" and, Msgr. Thomas McMahon, Secretary of the Catholic Near East Association, suggested that "[I] would prefer that all of [the shrines] be destroyed than the Christian population be eliminated." Andrej Kreutz, *Vatican Policy in the Palestinian–Israeli Conflict*, p. 99.

[37] "Civilta Cattolica: The Future of Jerusalem," p. 257. Israel is not a member of the UNESCO Convention. See text above, page 21.

[38] "Civilta Cattolica: The Future of Jerusalem," p. 259, note 21. This concern raises potential problems. The Vatican's concern is for a "living" city, one that maintains its holy and reverential quality. This "holy places plus" approach takes the Vatican far from its traditional spiritual role and may also reflect the need to treat the Christian demographic problem.

Finally, the Vatican believes that religious rights of freedom of religion and conscience must be preserved and protected. Optimally, the Vatican would insist on an international statutory instrument to achieve this goal.[39] Yet to a nuanced observer, it appears that the Vatican would be willing to consider the specific modalities of "bilateral plus." We must remember that most of this work has already been resolved in the Fundamental Agreement. Freedom of religion and conscience are protected by Article 1, sections 1 and 2. Indeed, in this area at least, there is little untrod ground for a new international agreement to cover. Some have suggested that were Israel to affirm existing international instruments (many of which it has already in fact affirmed), the required bow to the notion of international guarantees might well be met.[40] Some of these instruments include the November 25, 1981, UN Declaration on the Elimination of All Forms of Intolerance and of Discrimination Based on Religion or Belief,[41] the 1972 UNESCO Convention on the Protection of World Cultural and Natural Heritage,[42] and the 1976 Recommendation Concerning the Safeguarding and Contemporary Role of Historic Areas.[43] The exact modalities of such an arrangement, if any, will likely depend in large measure on the general state of Vatican–Israel relations at the time. To the extent that the Vatican's concerns regarding Jerusalem and the holy places are accomplished through the Fundamental Accord, the Vatican's need to "internationalize" issues related to Jerusalem will likely lessen.

---

[39] Indeed, the Vatican's current position seems to parallel its original message to the UN in 1979. See text above, p. 33, note 31.

[40] This is the personal view of Silvio Ferrari, as expressed in a letter to author, June 16, 1997. See also "Civilta Cattolica: The Future of Jerusalem," p. 257.

[41] *Yearbook of the United Nations* 35 (New York: United Nations, 1985), pp. 879-883.

[42] The Convention for the Protection of World Cultural and Natural Heritage, doc. no. 17 C/106, November 15, 1972, cited in *International Law Materials* 11 (1973), p. 1358.

[43] November 29, 1976, in UNESCO, *Conventions & Recommendations of UNESCO Concerning the Protection of the Cultural Heritage* (Geneva: UNESCO, 1985), p. 191.

V

The Interests of the Islamic Community

It must be recognized that the Arab interest in Jerusalem is not solely a Palestinian interest. The Israeli–Jordanian peace treaty states that "Israel respects the present special role of the Hashemite Kingdom of Jordan in Moslem holy shrines in Jerusalem. When negotiations on the permanent status takes place, Israel will give high priority to Jordan's historic roles in these shrines."[1] Although this should not be overinterpreted, it does indicate what ought in some sense to be obvious—that there are various formulations by which the Hashemite Kingdom might well keep a foothold in Jerusalem by meeting the religious, if not national, needs of the Arab world.

Palestinian–Jordanian rivalry over the holy places has intensified. In early December 1994, Faisal Husayni visited Jordan to discuss Jerusalem-related issues; at the conclusion of his visit he reported,

> We know full well that the holy places have been placed under Jordanian administrative guardianship. This situation has been recognized and accepted by Israel since 1967. We are not interested now in changing the situation. We agreed to discuss the status of Jerusalem with Israel in the second stage. We are not ready to open this file before the beginning of the official talks. Therefore, we believe that Jordan considers the holy places a trust that will be turned over to the Palestinians when they become capable of shouldering this responsbility. We agreed to maintain the situation as it is and to hold further coordination so that we will not make any wrong moves. . . . The matter is not one of sensitivities toward the Jordanian stand. However, in the absence of coordination, even the steps that are taken with good intentions might be misinterpreted by this or that party.[2]

Later that month the "action" shifted to the Islamic Conference in Casablanca. The Islamic Conference is a unique grouping of states with extensive Muslim populations who meet to discuss problems of the Muslim faith that cut across political boundaries (in contrast to the Arab League, which deals with political issues).[3] Morocco's King Hassan II, who himself claims descent from the prophet

---

[1] Israel–Jordan Peace Treaty, October 26, 1994, in *International Legal Materials* 34 (1995), pp. 43–48. This principle was first articulated in the so-called Washington Declaration of July 25, 1994. See Meron Medzini, ed., *Israel's Foreign Relations: Selected Documents 1992–1994* (Jerusalem: Ministry of Foreign Affairs of Israel, 1995), p. 716.

[2] Menachem Klein, "The Islamic holy places as a Political Bargaining Card (1993–1995)," *Catholic University Law Review* 45 (1996), p. 753.

[3] The Organization of the Islamic Conference (OIC) was formally established in May 1971 and currently has 52 member states. Pursuant to its charter the OIC has seven aims: promote Islamic solidarity among member states; consolidate cooperation among member states in economic,

Muhammad, heads the conference's Jerusalem Committee. There can be little doubt that the Jerusalem Committee will seek to involve itself in matters spiritual pertaining to Jerusalem. Thus, while Saudi Arabia and Morocco support Palestinian claims to political sovereignty in Jerusalem, they have not recognized Arafat's spiritual control.

At the conference, Jordan sought to mobilize support for a resolution recognizing it as the patron of the holy sites in Jerusalem. Jordan had wanted such a resolution to underscore the King's historical role as caretaker or trustee of the holy places. The PLO opposed this and the summit concluded with no mention of Jordan's role in protecting Arab interests.[4]

After the Casablanca meeting, Jordan agreed that it would "turn over custodianship of holy sites in Jerusalem to the Palestinians when the final status of the city has been determined in negotiations," but Amman has continued to assert its interest in the holy sites.[5] Still refusing to promote Jordanian interests, the Islamic Conference's Jerusalem Committee, meeting in Ifrane, Morocco, in January 1995, supported transferring power over the holy places to the PA.[6]

At the same time neither the Islamic Conference nor its Jerusalem Committee proposed what Jordan most feared—the creation of an Administrative Council of an amalgam of Islamic states to protect the holy places during the interim period. With the signing of a cooperation accord with Jordan in January 1995, the Palestinian rift with Jordan was papered over, at least officially. The accord affirms Jordan's support for the Palestinian people, under the leadership of the PLO, to win its right of self-determination over its territory and to establish an independent Palestinian state with Jerusalem as capital.

Notwithstanding their public rhetoric, it remains an open question whether "any of the Arab States would assume responsibility for the holy places in Jerusalem."[7] When Israeli deputy foreign minister Yossi Beilin sent envoys to explore this issue, an Israeli diplomatic source recalls, "We sat with the Saudis, we asked, 'Are you willing to take responsibility for the Temple Mount?' They

---

social, cultural, scientific and international affairs; eliminate racial segregation and discrimination; support international peace and security; coordinate all efforts to safeguard the Holy Places and support the struggle of the people of Palestine; strengthen the struggle of all Muslim people; and create an atmosphere for the promotion of cooperation and understanding among member states and other countries. The OIC is headquartered in Jiddah rather than Mecca to reflect the OIC's diplomatic rather than religious character. See "Organization of the Islamic Conference," in *The Middle East and North Africa* 43 (London: Europa Publications Limited, 1997), pp. 234–236; Martin S. Kramer, *An Introduction to World Islamic Conferences* (paper) (Tel Aviv: Shiloah Center for Middle Eastern and African Studies, Tel Aviv University, June 1978), pp. 30–33.

[4] In a snit, King Hussein left the Conference early. See "Hussein, Mubarak Discuss Jerusalem," *Jerusalem Post*, January 15, 1995, p. 1.

[5] See "Hussein Abruptly Leaves Islamic Summit," *Jerusalem Post*, December 15, 1994, p. 1.

[6] See Ali Bouzerda, "Moslems to Demand Palestinian Control of Jerusalem," *Reuters World Service*, January 17, 1995.

[7] Steve Rodman and Bill Hutman, "Of Talks and Traps," *Jerusalem Post*, May 3, 1996, p. 8.

said 'No, only if all the Arabs agree.' Who's left? Jordan now doesn't want Jerusalem. Morocco is too far."[8]

The Israeli assertion that Jordan does not want responsibility for the holy places in Jerusalem surely goes too far. In February 1995, in an interview with the Egyptian newspaper *al-Ahram*, King Hussein noted,

> I am who is responsible to the Arab side of the city. It was clearly stated in the UN decision 242. In accordance with the Israeli–Palestinian accords, the issue of Jerusalem is left to the final status negotiations. The Western side of the city has been the capital of the state of Israel since the day it was founded, but the Arab side could be a symbol of peace between both sides, and the sides will have to reach the suitable solution about Jerusalem. The issue of the holy sites of the city is a different matter that should be dealt with. Again, I want to reiterate that we the Hashemites and Jordanians have no intention in Jerusalem or wherever related to it. . . [W]e shall continue to bear that responsibility over the holy sites until a reasonable solution will be found.[9]

The spiritual card, after all, may be the last one that the king has to play. Still, there is little doubt that he intends to play it strongly. As his speech from the throne marking the opening of parliament on November 29, 1997, made clear, Jordan envisions a long-term role for itself in the holy places, suggesting that the holy places should be "above the sovereign considerations of any state."[10]

In an open letter to his prime minister, Abdul Salem al Majali, Hussein reinforced this view, pointing out that "Jordan will continue to demand special status with regard to Islamic holy places in Jerusalem and that this demand has no bearing on the Palestinian demand that Jerusalem be the capital of their future state."[11]

A TALE OF TWO *MUFTIS*

However weak its hand, Jordan has played it to the best of its ability. In August 1988, Jordan gave up any territorial claims to the West Bank. Nonetheless, it still kept up its ties with the area. Although it stopped paying the salaries of former

---

[8] Ibid.

[9] Col. Samuel Segev, "The Islamic–Religious Aspect in Jerusalem towards the Diplomatic Negotiations on the Issue of Jerusalem" (Jerusalem: Institute for National Security, July 1995), pp. 16–17 (Hebrew).

Still, it is not suprising, as only a year earlier King Hussein called for a "dialogue among the adherents of the divine faiths, preceded by a dialogue among the Moslem sects, which would unify their position and lead to brotherly relations among the faithful, as decreed by God when He made Jerusalem the object of their reverence. . . . As to custody over Jerusalem, this can only be the prerogative of Almighty God. Nor is there in any of this any diminution of the rights of the Palestinians to Jerusalem." King Hussein, cited in "Monarch slams 'intellectual terror' by Islamists and 'ungrateful' PLO challenge to religious link with Jerusalem," *Mideast Mirror* 8, 1994, p. 13.

[10] Robert Satloff, "The King is Back . . . and 'Final Status Talks' May Be Just Around the Corner," Washington Institute for Near East Policy, *PeaceWatch* 140, December 10, 1997.

[11] Ze'ev Schiff, "King Hussein's Letter," *Ha'aretz*, December 17, 1997, p. B1 (Hebrew).

Jordanian officials in the West Bank (as it had continued to do after the 1967 War) it continued to pay the salaries of Muslim religious functionaries[12] and to pay for renovations and restorations to the al-Aqsa mosque.[13] In September 1994, however, it severed its connections with all West Bank religious institutions. Still, the Hashemites continued to pay for religious functionaries in Jerusalem.[14] Picking up the "slack," the PA created a Ministry of Religious Affairs to govern the Muslim waqfs.[15] The PA now pays around $9 million to $11 million each year for the 2,000 to 2,500 waqf employees in the rest of the West Bank.

In Jerusalem, therefore, there are now two waqf administrations, one Jordanian and one Palestinian, each competing for authority over the Muslim holy places. At present, Jordan controls the waqf office in the Haram and both sides have promoted their own officials for various religious offices. Much of this is symbolic, however, because Sheikh Hassan Tahboub, the PA minister of the waqf and religious affairs, was previously a Jordanian waqf official and enjoys good relations with both sides. Indeed, Tahboub also serves as the president of the Supreme Muslim Council[16] and this double title provides him protection from Israeli charges that Tahboub, as a PA official, is operating illegally in Jerusalem under the Oslo Accord. In the West Bank, Tahboub acts as PA minister of religious affairs, whereas in Jerusalem he represents the Supreme Muslim Council, which is not technically a PA institution. To most Palestinians, however, he speaks in the name of the PA, even in Jerusalem.

---

[12] The costs of administering the Temple Mount and the waqf traditionally have been borne in large part by the Jordanian government. Between 1979 and 1988, approximately $10 million was transferred by Jordan to the waqf committee for general purposes. See Michael Dumper, *The Politics of Jerusalem*, p. 307, note 57. Other figures show $7 million contributed by Jordan and almost $21 million from other Arab groups for the preservation of the holy places between 1967 and 1987; Ibid., at Table 6.1, note 178. Yitzhak Reiter tells that Jordan spent $18 million in the early 1990s to subsidize the waqf, which was the largest employer in Arab Jerusalem. See Yitzhak Reiter, "Muslim Charitable Trusts in Jerusalem," *Israel Studies,* no. 5 (Winter 1992), p. 31.

Hassan Tahboub, the PA minister of religion, has pointed out that the Supreme Muslim Council's "budget had always required massive infusions of funds from Jordan." He estimated that the income from endowments and entrance fees "amounted to no more than 20 percent of their budget." Roger Friedland and Richard Hecht, *To Rule Jerusalem* (Cambridge: Cambridge University Press, 1996), p. 521, note 12.

[13] In December, 1996, Jordan purchased 2,000 square meters of carpets for al-Aqsa as a sign of its strengthened commitment to the Haram. "King Husayn donates carpets to Al-Aksa Mosque," *BBC Summary of World Broadcasts*, December 12, 1996.

[14] Jon Immanual, "Jordan renounces religious links to area," *Jerusalem Post*, September 28, 1994, p. 1.

[15] Idem., "Palestinian Authority Set Up Its Own *Waqf,*" *Jerusalem Post*, August 15, 1994, p. 2, and "The PA in Jerusalem," *Jerusalem Post*, March 8, 1995, p. 8. The PA's responsibility includes some 800 mosques, the *shari'a* (religious law) courts, and the local waqf offices throughout the West Bank. See Samuel Segev, "The Islamic–Religious Aspect in Jerusalem towards the Diplomatic Negotiations on the Issue of Jerusalem," p. 20.

[16] Jon Immanuel, "The PA in Jerusalem," p. 6.

This religio-nationalist competition has created a competition between two *muftis*, or government-appointed Islamic leaders, one Jordanian and one Palestinian. When the highly respected Sheikh Sa'ad al-Din al-'Alami died in 1993, both Jordan and the PA appointed successors, each claiming the mufti's mantle.[17] Thus far, although Israel has recognized Jordan's "special role" in the holy places,[18] the local community follows the rulings of the mufti appointed by the PA. Indeed, at the instructions of the PA, few Muslims ever enter the office of the "Jordanian mufti" in the Haram.

Tension, however, continues to bubble up. In April 1996, the PA ousted Sheikh Ansari, a Jordanian official, from his post as *rais al-sadana* (president of the Servants of al-Aqsa), replacing him with Khalil Alameh, a PA loyalist.[19] In August 1996, Jordan appointed Izat Duffash to be director of the al-Aqsa mosque. He now competes with Mohammed Hussein, the PA director who is staying on in Jerusalem.[20]

Recently, the PA and Jordan agreed to coordinate their religious activities in Jerusalem. Jordan agreed to pay for the waqf and to coordinate with the PA on decisions pertaining to religious sites.[21] This occurred after a confrontation on the Haram in October 1997 between waqf officials loyal to Jordan and those loyal to the PA.[22] Throughout 1997, however, the PA moved to take over the Islamic inistitutions in the Old City. An internal memorandum from Israeli prime minister Binyamin Netanyahu's office reported that Minister Tahboub "does not try and cover himself anymore as chairman of the Supreme Islamic Council, but operates openly as [waqf] and religous affairs minister for the PA."[23]

---

[17] President Clinton learned first-hand of this competition during his 1994 visit to Israel, when he "ditched a late night visit to the Old City rather than choose between two *muftis* at the gate to the Haram." Jon Immanuel, "Clinton Sidesteps Two-Headed Mufti," *Jerusalem Post*, October 28, 1994, p. 2A. A second reason for canceling the trip to the Old City was the insistence of Jerusalem mayor Ehud Olmert that he accompany Clinton into eastern Jerusalem, a practice frowned upon by the State Department.

[18] Israel–Jordan Peace Treaty, October 26, 1994, in *International Legal Materials* 34 (1995), pp. 43–48.

[19] Bill Hutman, "Ousted *Waqf* Official Detained in Jericho," *Jerusalem Post*, April 18, 1996, p. 3.

[20] Interestingly, Duffash took a leave of absence immediately after his appointment. See, Bill Hutman, "Jordan Names New Al-Aksa Director; PA Keeps Old One," *Jerusalem Post*, August 19, 1996, p. 2.

[21] "Palestinian–Jordanian Agreement on holy places in Jerusalem," *Deutsche Presse-Agentur*, November 7, 1996; Bill Hutman, "PA, Jordanian *Waqf*s Meet," *Jerusalem Post*, November 5, 1996, p. 2; Bill Hutman, "PA Says It Won't Try to Control *Waqf*," *Jerusalem Post*, November 7, 1996, p. 2.

[22] David Makovsky, "Netanyahu Phones Arafat over *Waqf* Power Struggle," *Jerusalem Post*, October 27, 1996, p. 2.

[23] Elli Wohlgelernter, "Gov't Memo: PA Becoming Islamic Guardian in Jerusalem," *Jerusalem Post,* September 29, 1997, p. 2.

THE TEMPLE MOUNT: A SPECIAL CHALLENGE

Israel has faced a formidable challenge with respect to Muslim holy places. Immediately after the military victory in 1967, many Jews assumed the Temple Mount was "liberated" and would become a place of Jewish worship. Then–Defense Minister Moshe Dayan, however, decreed that the Temple Mount area was off limits for Jewish worship and that Muslim religious officials were free to organize and administer worship at the mosques as before. Dayan's ruling was in accord with standard *halachic* (Jewish ritual law) practice, which prohibits Jews from setting foot on the Temple Mount for fear of treading on and thereby desecrating the holy ground where the Holy of Holies once stood.[24] Nonetheless, its purpose was not religious but prudential. Given the harsh treatment accorded by Muslims to Jews at the Western Wall during the Mandatory period and before, one might well have expected a retaliatory approach. Dayan's decision spoke volumes of wisdom.[25]

The Western Wall is located at the base of what Jews refer to as the Temple Mount (or Har HaBayit), the site of King Solomon's and King Herod's Temples.[26] The Temple Mount has been considered of supreme holiness to Jews since the building of the first Temple. Indeed, Jewish tradition accepts it as the site of the binding of Isaac by Abraham. The Western Wall is therefore a place of extreme holiness to Jews, the sole remaining remnant of Temple architecture (the retaining wall) from which, as Rav Aha in the *midrash*[27] noted, the *shechinah* (spirit of God) has never departed.

---

[24] The prohibition is found in the *Shulchan Aruch, Orah Hayim,* at section 562 (the *Shulchan Aruch* is the authoritative code of Jewish law written by Joseph Caro in the sixteenth century). Most of the religious sources follow Maimonides on forbidding entry onto the Temple Mount. (See Mishneh Torah, Hilchot Bet ha-Behirah 6:15-16). See Magen Avraham (on Orah Hayim 561:62), Biur ha-Gra (on Yoreh-De'ah 331:6) and Mishnah Berurah (on Orah Hayim 561:5). There is a question as to whether Rabbi Abraham ben David of Posquieres (known as the Ravad), a famous twelfth century Talmudic authority, considered that the Temple Mount lost its sanctity after the destruction and that therefore the prohibition does not apply. Most authorities, however, do not interpret the Ravad in this way.

[25] Meron Benvenisti describes Moshe Dayan's decision, in *City of Stone: The Hidden History of Jerusalem*, p. 73.

[26] Ownership of the Wall remains a sensitive issue between Jews and Muslims because of the historic Muslim fear that Jews may use the Western Wall to enter the Temple Mount. Shlomo Berkovitz, explaining Israel's 1968 expropriation of the Jewish Quarter and Mugrabi Gate to build the Western Wall Plaza, has concluded that "in the map of the expropriation order, and I'm not sure how this happened, the bottom meter of the Wall, that is, its base, is included for the length of 140 meters, which includes all the prayer space at the foot of the Wall and the archeological excavations there. However, legally and formally, the remaining portion of the Wall still belongs to the Waqf," quoted in Aryeh Dean Cohen, "Whose Wall Is It, Anyway?" *Jerusalem Post*, November 21, 1997, p. 3.

[27] The *midrash* is a collection of rabbinical works containing ethical lessons derived from scriptural verses.

The Western Wall was the site of Jewish worship during the early period of Islamic rule of Palestine. Ottoman governing authorities continued to grant Jews the privilege (if not the right) of worshiping at the Wall, and taxed them for that privilege, because the Wall—including the Mugrabi Quarter adjacent to it—was recognized under Ottoman law to be waqf property.

The Temple Mount is known to Muslims as the Haram al-Sharif, "the Noble Enclosure,"[28] in which stand two of Islam's most treasured monuments: The Dome of the Rock shrine, marking the site of Muhammad's heavenly ascent, and the Mosque of al-Aqsa, which is the central place of congregational prayer for Muslims throughout the country. As a matter of historical record, the Temple Mount was barred to non-Muslims until early in the nineteenth century. A few travelers succeeded in gaining entry from the early 1830s and Sir Moses Montefiore, a nineteenth century English philanthropist, went up the Temple Mount in 1855, arousing much Rabbinic displeasure.[29] After the Crimean War, non-Muslims were allowed entry after paying a tax and receiving a special permit.[30] Since 1967 non-Muslims have been allowed to visit except during periods of Muslim prayer, when only Muslims are allowed on the Haram. Indeed, Muslim tradition militates against a non-Muslim praying in a mosque and argues that "the whole of the Noble Sanctuary is a mosque, including its empty spaces."[31] More forcefully, Sheikh Sa'ad al-Din al-'Alami, the late head of the

---

[28] A beautiful introduction is to be found in Alistair Duncan, *The Noble Sanctuary: Portrait of A Holy Place in Arab Jerusalem* (London: Longman Group, 1972).

[29] Montefiore's supporters claimed that he was relying on the opinion of the Ravad permitting entry. See A. Schischa, "The Saga of 1855: A Study in Depth" in Sonia and V. D. Lipman, eds., *The Century of Moses Montefiore* (New York: Oxford University Press, 1985), p. 269, 306.

[30] See generally, Yehoshua Ben-Arieh, *Jerusalem in the Nineteenth century: the Old City* (New York: St. Martin's Press, 1984), p. 141–148. In the 1920s the *mufti* opened a museum on the Haram and cleared it of the poor who lived there. Tourists regularly visited except during the hours of prayer.

[31] The words are those of the late Anwar Nuseibeh and are cited in E. Offenbacher, "Prayer in the Temple Mount," *Jerusalem Quarterly* 36 (Summer 1985), pp. 128, 134.

As a matter of Islamic religious law the issue of entry of nonbelievers such as Jews or Christians into mosques is somewhat unclear. There does not appear to be any explicit textual reference in the Qur'an that forbids it.

The issue of nonbelievers *praying* on the Haram is even more complex. Muslim law forbids the ritually impure from praying in a mosque. Nonbelievers are likely to be ritually impure and therefore are forbidden from participating in prayer. Yet, at least one Islamic scholar, Abdul Hadi Palazzi, takes the position that "there is no prohibition in Islam or in the Koran against Jewish prayer on the Temple Mount. The prohibition is against prayer in the Dome of the Rock and in the Al-Aqsa Mosque," which take up only a portion of the Temple Mount. See Nadav Shragai, "What is allowed to Muslims in Europe," *Ha'aretz*, July 18, 1996, p. B2 (Hebrew). A more general formulation that Islam ought to respect Jewish worship (and indeed Jewish sovereignty) in Jerusalem can be found in Abdul Hadi Palazzi, "Jerusalem: A Triple Religious Heritage for a Contemporary Single Administration," paper delivered at a conference on *Jerusalem: City of Law and Justice*, Jerusalem, July 1996. Palazzi's views on Jewish worship on the Haram are clearly

Supreme Muslim Council in eastern Jerusalem, vowed that "Muslims will never permit any Jew to pray" on the Temple Mount.[32]

To further complicate matters, the Western Wall is also revered by Muslims as the place where Muhammad tethered his horse, *al-Buraq* (Lightning), before his heavenly ascent. Just as the Western Wall has emerged as a powerful nationalistic expression for many Israelis, so the Haram al-Sharif has become for Muslims a symbol of their own nationalistic feelings about Jerusalem and Palestine.

Israeli law concerning the Temple Mount is particularly confusing.[33] Israel claims sovereignty over the Temple Mount, but has chosen *de facto* to allow the waqf to control day-to-day activity on the Mount absent any breakdown of public order.[34] Further, the government often uses its discretion not to enforce regulatory requirements—such as those for building permits and laws related to the protection of archeological sites.[35]

For its part, the waqf officially refuses to accept Israeli authority. It does not, for example, ordinarily defend itself in court cases,[36] nor does it apply for construction permits or do anything that openly suggests acceptance of Israeli sovereignty. Yet the notion of waqf "sovereignty" over the Haram is largely fiction. Unofficially, waqf officials meet with Israeli officials on a daily basis. Israeli police maintain a substation on the Temple Mount, next to waqf offices. Together with waqf guards, they routinely stand at the gates to the Mount. In

---

idiosyncratic and do not appear to be followed by other authorities. The authors have benefited from conversations with Prof. Ifrah Zilberman on these issues.

[32] Ian S. Lustick, *For the Land and the Lord: Jewish Fundamentalism in Israel* (New York: Council on Foreign Relations Press, 1988), p. 128.

[33] The leading articles in English include Shmuel Berkovitz, "The Holy Places in Jerusalem: Legal Aspects," *Justice,* no. 11 (1996), pp. 4–14, and "The Holy Places in Jerusalem: Legal Aspects (Part Two)," *Justice,* no. 12 (1997), pp. 17–21; Asher Maoz, "Religious Human Rights in the State of Israel," in Johan D. van der Vyver and John Witte Jr., eds., *Religious Human Rights in Global Perspective: Legal Perspectives* 349 (Boston: Martinus Nijhoff, 1996), p. 349; Izhak England, "The Legal Status of the Holy Places in Jerusalem," *Israel Law Review* 28 (1994), p. 589; and Stephen J. Adler, "The Temple Mount in Court," *Biblical Archaeology Review* 17, no. 5 (September/October 1991), p. 60.

[34] The situation regarding the Christian holy places is similar. The official policy of the Israeli police is that they can enter a Christian holy place whenever the need arises. Yet, in practice, the police will only enter when they are either in hot pursuit or have obtained prior permission from a church official.

[35] See Justice Menachem Elon's majority opinion in HCJ 4185/90, *Temple Mount Faithful v. Attorney General*, 47(5) PD 221 (1993), translated in *Catholic University Law Review* 45 (1996), p. 861; see also HCJ 4935/93, *The Temple Mount Faithful v. The Mayor of Jerusalem*, 47(5) PD 865 (1993), which upheld the government's discretion regarding unlicensed construction work and allowing Arab youths to hold picnics and play ball games at archeological sites on the Haram; and most recently, Evelyn Gordon, "Court Asks State for Details in Temple Mount Construction," *Jerusalem Post*, September 25, 1996, p. 2.

[36] See, for example, *Temple Mount Faithful v. Attorney General.*

April 1997, a senior waqf official was put on trial in Jerusalem's district court for allegedly striking Jews on the Temple Mount.[37]

The recent construction of the mosque at Solomon's Stables is an example of how, contrary to public pronouncements, Israelis and waqf officials informally cooperate. Whereas the waqf publicly denied that Israel had any say on work at the site,[38] an antiquities authority official visited the construction site once a week. Old City police commander David Givati also visited regularly.[39]

The question of what legal rights, if any, Jews have to visit and pray on the Temple Mount is not just a perplexing legal question but one that has regularly triggered violent disturbances.[40] Under the Mandate, readers will recall, the issue was removed from the courts by the 1924 Order in Council and reserved for the political sphere. In a significant 1970 opinion, *Nationalist Circles Society v. Minister of Police*,[41] the Israeli Supreme Court ruled that the Mandatory order still applies if the dispute in question governs "substantive rights," but that disputes not relating to religious interests such as criminal acts—even those committed for religious purposes and intent—can be decided by the courts.[42]

In 1975, a group of young nationalistic Jews went on the Temple Mount for prayer and were arrested for disturbing the peace. A magistrate, Ruth Orr, acquitted them of charges and later "criticized the Ministry of Religious Affairs for not establishing regulations which would allow Jewish prayer on the Temple Mount."[43] Muslims took Magistrate Orr's ruling as legitimizing Jewish prayer on the Temple Mount. Suddenly there was a revival of the old charge of Jewish intentions to take over the Haram and raze the mosques and make room for the building of a third Jewish Temple. Then-Mayor Teddy Kollek and the Israeli government hastened to reassure Muslim authorities about the sanctity and security of the Haram, but with little effect. Although the decision was later reversed by the Israeli Supreme Court,[44] riots ensued and Arabs held their first

---

[37] The trial is noted in *Yated Ne'eman* (U.S. edition), April 18, 1997, p. 30.

[38] Similarly, whereas the waqf refuses to deal officially with Israeli authorities regarding road construction abutting Muslim cemeteries in eastern Jerusalem, the authors were assured by Israeli officials that waqf officials were in daily contact with the construction crew.

[39] Interview with William Hutman, February 2, 1997.

[40] The current question is reminiscent of the similar disturbances during the Mandate over control of the Western Wall. See text above, p. 9, and accompanying notes.

[41] HCJ 222/68, *Nationalist Circles Society v. Minister of Police*, 24(2) PD 141 (1970), excerpted in *Israel Yearbook of Human Rights* 20 (1990), p. 376.

[42] Claude Klein, "The Temple Mount Case," *Israel Law Review* 6 (1971), p. 257. See also HCJ 267/88, *Kolel Haidra and Rabbi Goren v. The State of Israel and the Court for Local Matters*, 43(3) PD 728 (1989).

[43] The affair is described in some detail in Walter Zander, "Truce on the Temple Mount," *New Outlook* 19 (July/August 1976), p. 14.

[44] See "Ban on Jewish Prayer at Temple Mount Upheld," *New York Times*, March 22, 1976, p. 4.

public demonstration since the Yom Kippur War, in the Damascus Gate area of the Old City.

From the perspective of legal doctrine—not public policy—the state of the law is, in some respects, unstable. In the *Nationalist Circles* case, Justice Simon Agranat attempted to sustain the analytic distinction between the right of access and the right to pray.[45] On this view, the freedom of access promised in the Protection of the Holy Places Law extends only to entry onto the Temple Mount but does not include the right to pray. Access is based on the above referenced statute which provides that "[t]he Holy Places shall be protected from desecration and any other violation and from anything likely to violate the freedom of access of the members of the different religions to the places sacred to them or their feelings with regard to those places."[46] Since the 1967 statute does not include prayer, that "right" is the business of the executive realm, not the courts. In the same case, Justice Alfred Witkin advanced an even more gossamer distinction, suggesting that the right of Jews to pray on the Temple Mount is certain, but, to quote Professor Claude Klein, "it does not follow from the existence of the right to hold prayers that there exists also a right to demand the active aid of the police in order to enforce it."[47]

As Justice Yitzhak England has suggested, the courts have begun to move from the denial of an enforceable right to pray on the Temple Mount to the recognition of an abstract right subject to the needs of public order.[48] Thus, in one recent case, *Gershon Solomon v. Yair Yitzchaki,* the Supreme Court wrote, "The petitioner, like any other person in Israel, enjoys the freedom of conscience, belief, religious observance and practice. This framework provides him with the privilege of gaining access to the Temple Mount for purposes of worship."[49] In principle, then, Jews have the right to pray on the Temple Mount.[50]

On this view, the law would ensure access contingent upon the executive (i.e., police) decision that doing so would not cause a breakdown in public

---

[45] HCJ 222/68, *Nationalist Circles Society v. Minister of Police,* 24(2) PD 141 (1970); see pp. 194–228 (J. Agranat).

[46] *The Protection of the Holy Places Law, 1967* is restated in the 1980 Jerusalem Basic Law; see *Basic Law: Jerusalem, Capital of Israel,* in LSI 34 (July 30, 1980), p. 209, sec. 3. Supporters of Jewish prayer on the Temple Mount argued that their freedom of access to the Temple Mount was violated.

[47] Claude Klein, "The Temple Mount Case," *Israel Law Review* 6 (1971), p. 263. See generally HCJ 222/68 *Nationalist Circles Society v. Minister of Police,* pp. 160–168 (J. Witkin).

[48] See Izhak England, "The Legal Status of the Holy Places in Jerusalem," *Israel Law Review* 28 (1994), pp. 596–597.

[49] HCJ 3374, *Gershon Solomon v. Yair Yitzchaki* (decided June 10, 1997) (Hebrew).

[50] There is a second technical legal issue: Is a decision to invoke the public order rule a reviewable act or one "committed to agency discretion?" The authors do not address this issue here. To the extent to which the issue of Jewish prayer on the Temple Mount is solely an executive decision, the executive branch can expect increasing political rhetoric (if not pressure) to relax its positions and allow some form of prayer.

order.[51] The question is, of course, what constitutes public order. The courts have generally taken a very deferential view of the term leaving it to the judgment of the police as experts. Thus, public order considerations have included not only exigencies of the moment (for example, the inability to protect worshippers at the time of the request), but also deference to police priorities regarding the deployment of their forces throughout the city.[52]

Within this legal context, two groups of orthodox Jews, the Temple Mount Faithful and Chai V'kayam, make recurrent efforts to ascend the Mount for prayer. The two groups differ markedly in their approach. The Faithful have always "been determined to obey the law and all the instructions from the Jerusalem police" engaging at most in "passive resistance."[53] Far more important, however, is the ultranationalist group Chai V'kayam, which has close contacts with both the settlers and the religious parties. Their leader, Yehuda Etzion, was convicted in the early 1980s of planning to blow up the Dome of the Rock, and many of his supporters come from the anti-Arab "underground" active in the 1980s.[54]

---

[51] In one recent case, the court gave approval for a group of ultranationalists, the Temple Mount Faithful, to visit the Temple Mount on *Tisha B'Av* (the fast day commemorating the Temple's destruction) "as long as they follow police instructions." See "Arab League condemns Israeli 'aggression' against Al-Aqsa," *Agence France Presse,* August 21, 1995; HCJ 4868/95, *Temple Mount Faithful v. Jerusalem Authorities and Israel Police* (decided August 3, 1995) (unpublished Hebrew). On another occasion, police announced they would allow small groups to enter as long as their presence "did not disturb public order or threaten security." The police allowed the religious activists to enter the Temple Mount in pairs, without their prayer books, but the Faithful tried to force their way in, in large numbers, by breaking through the gate; they were subsequently arrested. See Patricia Golan, "Israelis Arrested for Trying to Pray on Temple Mount," *Israel Faxx* 4, July 26, 1996; See also, Doug Struck, "Scuffles Lead to Closure of Religious Site in Jerusalem," *Baltimore Sun,* August 7, 1995, p. 3A.

[52] Yet, in an unusual reversal of a police assertion regarding public order, the "Faithful" were granted permission (after litigation) to pray at the nearby Mugrabi gate, which is an entrance to the Temple Mount. See HCJ 292/83, *The Temple Mount Faithful v. Jerusalem District Police Commander,* 38(2) PD 449 (1984), excerpted in *Israel Yearbook on Human Rights* 15 (1985), pp. 292–295.

[53] This said, it cannot be doubted that the "Faithful," led by Gershon Solomon, achieved media fame when their efforts to ascend the Mount sparked the 1989 Muslim riots. See Ehud Sprinzak, *The Ascendance of Israel's Radical Right* (New York: Oxford University Press, 1991), p. 280; see also Eliezer Don-Yehiya "The Book and the Sword: The Nationalist Yeshivot and Political Radicalism in Israel," in Martin E. Marty and R. Scott Appleby, eds., *Accounting for Fundamentalisms: The Dynamic Character of Movements* (Chicago: University of Chicago Press, 1994), p. 197.

[54] See Eliezer Don-Yehiya "The Book and the Sword," pp. 278, 282; Robert I. Friedman, *Zealots for Zion: Inside Israel's West Bank Movement* (New York: Random House, 1992), pp. 54–56; Ehud Sprinzak, *The Ascendancy of Israel's Radical Right,* pp. 252–261; Roger Friedland and Richard D. Hecht, "The Politics of Sacred Space: Jerusalem's Temple Mount/al-haram al-sharif," in Jamie Scott and Paul Simpson-Housley, eds., *Sacred Spaces and Profane Spaces: Essays in the Geographies of Judaism, Christianity, and Islam* (New York: Greenwood Press, 1991), pp. 52–53;

In what has become what some may call a seasonal ritual, both groups seek court approval, on a regular basis, to enter the Temple Mount on Jewish holidays,[55] on the Ninth of Av,[56] and on Jerusalem Day.[57] They have sought to revive the "first fruits" offerings on the intermediate days of Passover,[58] to blow shofar on the high holidays,[59] and to lay the cornerstone of the Third Temple.[60] Citing a potential threat to public order, the police generally reject all these efforts to secure access as a group.[61] Thus, public order considerations have meant that the police may, if they so judge it necessary, not only prohibit all Jews from access on specific days but even deny access to specific individuals.[62]

---

and Ian S. Lustick, *For the Land and the Lord: Jewish Fundamentalism in Israel* (New York: Council on Foreign Relations Press, 1988), pp. 69–70, 97–98, 168–176. A useful analysis of the political and religious conflict surrounding the Temple Mount can be found in Nadav Shragai, *The Temple Mount Conflict: Jews and Muslims, Religion and Politics Since 1967* (Jerusalem: Keter Publishing, 1995) (Hebrew).

[55] See, for example, HCJ 1663/94 *Gershon Solomon v. Givatz* (decided March 23, 1994) (unpublished Hebrew) (Pesach).

[56] See, for example, HCJ 4044/93, *Gershon Solomon v. Inspector General of Police* (decided February 20, 1996) (Hebrew); HCJ 3995/94, *Temple Mount Faithful v. Inspector General, Arye Amut, Comm. of Police* (decided July 14, 1994) (Hebrew).

[57] See, for example, HCJ 2725/93, *Gershon Solomon v. Inspector General of Police* (decided May 19, 1996) (Hebrew); HCJ 2592/94, *Temple Mount Faithful v. Minister of Police* (decided May 9, 1994) (Hebrew); HCJ 3374/97, *Gershon Solomon v. Yair Yitzhaki, Jerusalem Commander of Police* (decided June 10, 1997) (Hebrew); HCJ 292/83, *Temple Mount Faithful v. Jerusalem District Police Commander*, 38(2) PD 449 (1984), excerpted in *Israel Yearbook on Human Rights* 15 (1985), pp. 292–295, (request to pray at Mugrabi Gate allowed under conditions); and HCJ 3163/96, *Gershon Solomon v. Commander of Jerusalem District and Israel Police*, (decided May 14, 1996) (Hebrew) (request to enter Har HaBayit on Jerusalem Day denied).

[58] After being rebuffed, sheaves of wheat were deposited at the bottom of the Mughrabi Gate entrance to the Temple Mount; see Ron Kampeas, "Clash Connected to Faithful," *Jerusalem Post Magazine*, April 13, 1990, p. 2.

[59] This effort occurred at the end of Yom Kippur in 1981; see David Shipler, "In Old Jerusalem, Prayer can be an Incendiary Act," *New York Times*, October 20, 1981, p. A2.

[60] Haim Shapiro, "Temple Mount Faithful to Lay 'Cornerstone of Third Temple,'" *Jerusalem Post*, October 11, 1989, p. 1.

[61] In HCJ 67/93, *Kach Movement v. Minister of Religious Affairs*, 47(2) PD 1 (1990), excerpted in *Israel Yearbook on Human Rights* 20 (1990), p. 376, for example, the police claimed that there was a risk that access would be seen as provacatory and lead to bloodshed.

[62] "Israeli commander bans "right wing activists" from Temple Mount," *BBC Summary of World Broadcasts*, November 18, 1997. For example in HCJ 3374/97, *Gershon Solomon v. Yair Yitzhaki, Jerusalem Commander of Police*, (decided June 10, 1997) (unpublished Hebrew), an Israeli police chief testified, in an effort to prevent Solomon going onto Temple Mount on Jerusalem Day, that "our assessment is that provative ascent of the petitioner to the Temple Mount and especially during Jerusalem Day will most probably create sufficient friction causing disturbance of public order and endangering the safety of visitors and worshippers in the area." The Court found that "when there is a high probability of public safety risk if this privilege [access] is granted, it is justified not to grant this privilege."

On occasion, members of these groups are allowed to enter the Temple Mount individually or in small groups of up to five after their identity cards are checked.[63] If any of the Faithful show evidence of prayer while standing on the Har HaBayit, however, they are physically removed.[64]

Although the symbolic content associated with the Temple Mount makes this deference to public order understandable, conceptually it is hard to state that a right to pray exists but can never be actualized because of a fear for public safety. If a right is regularly and continuously denied (albeit for good and sufficient reasons in each case), it is hard to continue articulating it as a "right."[65]

Substantial issues, moreover, remain in classifying what counts as prayer. Silent prayer, of course, is a private act and not observably distinguishable from a meditative visit (i.e. access). Until recently, it was agreed that Jews can enter the Temple Mount to visit individually or to pray silently.[66] Public prayer is something else entirely, in particular because in Judaism, public prayer is most often organized in a group setting with the use of religious paraphernalia, such as *tallit, tefillin,* or *sifrei torah.* Further, as one cannot easily decide if an individual is praying or merely looking contemplative, the practical result has been a ban on any outward manifestation of individual prayer as well as on group prayer. Thus, the Israeli Supreme Court has consistently held that individuals seeking access to the Temple Mount could not pray publicly, carry a prayer book, or wear any religious apparel.[67]

The clear issue of whether individual prayer is, by definition, a violation of public order did rise in July 1997 when a Jerusalem magistrate court authorized Chai V'kayam leader Yehuda Etzion to pray on the Temple Mount "as long as he

---

[63] Thus one frustrated "worshiper" commented that entering was like "crossing a foreign border"; see Elli Wohlgelernter, "Old City Celebration has Extra Kick," *Jerusalem Post*, June 5, 1997, p. 2.

[64] On one occasion a member of such a group shouted the words of the *shema* (a Hebrew prayer) three times and was evicted. Dan Izenberg, "Tight Security for Visit by Temple Mount Faithful," *Jerusalem Post*, April 24, 1989, p. 10.

[65] This would certainly be an American view of the matter. This line of reasoning is dismissed in HCJ 4044/93, *Gershon Solomon v. Inspector General of Police* (decided February 20, 1996) (unpublished Hebrew); HCJ 2725/93, *Gershon Solomon v. Inspector General of Police* (decided May 19, 1996) (unpublished Hebrew). Both cases denied access to petitioners. In the first case, Deputy President Levin dissented, suggesting that "the right to worship and freedom of speech have such power that whoever is claiming it ought to expect that the state will undertake the necessary means in order that an offence to this right will be thwarted."

[66] HCJ 99/76, *Cohen v. The Minister of Police,* 30(2) PD 505. Such access has been denied to groups like the Temple Mount Faithful who allegedly sought access to demonstrate or pray. See, for example, the denial of access to the "Faithful" on Jerusalem Day in the many cases cited in note 57.

[67] See also HCJ 67/93, *Kach Movement v. Minister of Religious Affairs,* 47(2) PD 1 (1990), excerpted in *Israel Yearbook on Human Rights* 20 (1990), p. 376. See also Asher Maoz, "Religious Human Rights in the State of Israel," pp. 383–384.

came alone, did not wear a prayer shawl, and 'murmured' his prayer so as not to disturb Moslem worshipers."[68]

After a hurried police request for clarification, Judge Amnon Cohen underscored that he had not intended to break new ground—that is, he had not intended to change the analytic balance between the individual right of access and the state's prerogative to protect public order. As he saw it, murmuring prayer would not "reasonably" disturb the Muslims and the public order rule thus would not apply. The result was a rerun of past efforts to change the status quo. Etzion arrived with a group, sought entry, and the police invoked the public order exemption.[69] But what of the next case? Once the matter becomes a judicial not an executive matter and a legal right to pray is found, the distinctions advanced by the court become difficult to sustain.

The Temple Mount/Haram issue has continued to engender violence. Since 1967, the few hundred square meters the holy site occupies have witnessed arson and murder. In 1969, as mentioned above, Denis Michael Rohan set fire to the mosque, and in 1982, an American Jew wearing an Israeli uniform, Alan Goodman, opened fire on worshipers at the mosque. In 1984, Israeli security organizations foiled a conspiracy by a Jewish ultranationalist underground to destroy the Muslim shrines on the Temple Mount.[70]

During the 1980s, Muslim groups began to use the Temple Mount as a focal point for religious figures seeking to infuse nationalism with religious sentiments. Incendiary pamphlets were distributed and sermons often provoked clashes with police. Increased Muslim Brotherhood influence in the Jordanian waqf administration seemed to exacerbate this problem,[71] as did the intifada, which began in 1987. On April 7, 1989, a group of Muslims threw rocks from the Haram into the Western Wall Plaza.[72] Two weeks later, the deputy mufti, Sheikh Mohammed al-Jamal, ignoring a police crackdown on the number of worshipers to the holy site, called for mass prayer demonstrations.[73]

Incendiary rhetoric at sermons increased over the following year. Fearful that the "Temple Mount Faithful" were planning an assault on the Haram, al-Jamal

---

[68] "Jewish extremists arrested for trying to pray at Al Aksa," *Agence France Presse*, July 27, 1997.

[69] Ibid., See also "Police Detain Etzion, Two Others on Temple Mount," *Jerusalem Post*, July 28, 1997, p. 3.

[70] See text above, p. 25, and accompanying notes.

[71] Ifrah Zilberman, "The Temple Mount: Jordan's Changing Role," *Jerusalem Post*, November 7, 1990, p. 6.

[72] Israeli police officials blamed the riot on Hamas activists. See Daniel Williams, "Muslims, Israel Police Clash at Islamic Holy Site," *Los Angeles Times*, April 8, 1989, p. 14.

[73] Al-Jamal called on Muslims to "perform Friday prayers at Al-Aqsa mosque" and stated that "if the Israeli authorities prevent them from entering the mosque, they are to pray in the Old City of Jerusalem. If they are barred from entering the city, they are to pray on the roads leading to Jerusalem." Dan Izenberg, "Moslems Urged to Flock to Al-Aqsa," *Jerusalem Post*, April 21, 1989, p. 18.

called for all Muslims in both Israel and the territories to gather and defend the Haram against alleged Jewish incursions.[74] The resulting melee led, in quick order, from stone throwing to riot to death. Nineteen Arabs were killed and more than one-hundred fifty wounded when Israeli border police clashed with stone throwers on October 8, 1990.[75] It was the worst bloodshed in Jerusalem since 1967.

More violence ensued in early October 1996 when Israel opened a second exit to a Hasmonean tunnel that had been dug along the side of the Temple Mount from the Western Wall Plaza.[76] The opening of this exit was viewed by Palestinians as a provocation that sparked a week of rioting throughout the West Bank and Gaza, leaving more than seventy dead and hundreds wounded. Although much of the conflict was clearly manipulated by PA leader Yasir Arafat for political purposes, there can be no doubt that the accusation, however fanciful, that the tunnel opening was a first step to Israeli takeover of the Temple Mount struck an intense and responsive chord with Palestinian Muslims.

In October 1996, the waqf opened a new mosque on the Haram for worship. It is situated underground in Solomon's Stables, which is part of the structure built during Herodian times but later, during the Crusades, became associated with King Solomon.[77] Some have claimed that the waqf had reached an agreement with the previous Labor government that the mosque, named the Marwani Mosque, could be opened in return for the opening by Israel of a second exit to the Hasmonean tunnel. The waqf denied any such agreement. The Labor government had given permission for the mosque to be used intermittently during Ramadan and on rainy days when worshipers could not pray in the al-Aqsa courtyard. The waqf, for its part, argued that Israeli permission was not necessary. The Supreme Court again refused to intervene in the waqf's decisions, while reserving the authority to do so should the occasion arise.[78] And although

---

[74] Ibid. The call to gather at the al-Aqsa Mosque came two weeks prior to a clash during a sermon at the Mosque. See Daniel Williams, "How the Fuse of Jerusalem's Religious Rivalry Was Lit at Temple Mount," *Los Angeles Times*, October 15, 1990, p. A8. Shortly after the riots, al-Jamal was remanded into custody. "Court Extends Detentions of Sheikh Jamal Hussaini," *Jerusalem Post*, October 21, 1990, p. 4.

[75] Jackson Diehl, "Israeli Police Kill 19 Palestinians in Temple Mount Confrontation," *Washington Post*, October 9, 1990, p. A1.

[76] The Hasmonean tunnel is not a holy site. It only provides access to another tunnel that runs along the Temple Mount, which is a holy site. Allowing the Hasmonean tunnel to be recognized as a holy site would justify claims that the project was damaging the Mount when, in reality, it is only a secondary access tunnel to the Mount.

[77] Bill Hutman, "Government Allows *Waqf* to Open Solomon's Stables for Muslim Worshipers," *Jerusalem Post*, October 10, 1996, p. 1.

[78] See "Israeli Court rules Muslim Prayer at Solomon's Stables Legal," *BBC Summary of World Broadcasts*, March 14, 1997. See also HCJ 5410/97, *Chai V'kayam Movement v. Attorney General* (decided October 30, 1997) (Hebrew), where petitioners asked the court to order the pulling-up of new flooring laid down in the Solomon's Stables mosque as the work was allegedly done in

Attorney General Elyakim Rubenstein reportedly accused waqf authorities of planning illegal construction and expansion projects at the Marwani Mosque, the government used its discretion not to stop the renovation work.[79]

---

violation of planning and building antiquities legislation. The court rejected the petition noting that "it is well known that this court has determined in a significant number of decisions that it does not tend to interfere in decisions of the government, the Attorney General or the Municipality concerning the issue of the law of Har HaBayit. These things are known and there is no need to go back and review the decisions."

[79] See "Israeli report says Palestinians 'expanding activities' on Temple Mount," *BBC Summary of World Broadcasts,* October 18, 1997; see also "New Troubles brewing over Palestinian building at Al-Aqsa mosque," *Agence France Presse,* October 14, 1997; "Israeli decides not to stop Temple Mount Work 'at this stage,'" *BBC Summary of World Broadcasts,* October 16, 1997; and Elli Wohlgelernter, "Wakf Not Building on Temple Mount," *Jerusalem Post,* October 27, 1997, p. 2. Waqf officials argued that they were merely repairing, not expanding, and that the aluminum kiosk they were building at the mosque's entrance was removable and not a permanent structure; "New troubles brewing over Palestinian building at Al-Aqsa mosque," *Agence France Presse,* October 14, 1997.

VI

The Interests of the Jewish Community

The problem of sites holy to more than one religion is particularly vexing. The various resolutions of the competing claims to the Cave of Machpaleh in Hebron have proved consistently unstable. Dwarfing this, of course, are the competing claims of Jews and Muslims to the holiness of the Temple Mount.

Many orthodox Jews see control of the Temple Mount or Har HaBayit as central to the Messianic Age. "The yearning for the Temple," Knesset Member Hanan Porat has suggested, "is longing for the renewal of a dialogue between God and Israel."[1] At the same time, others believe that Har HaBayit is key to the religious nationalist project of a greater land of Israel (Eretz Yisrael HaShlaymah). Indeed Gershon Solomon, leader of the Temple Mount Faithful, has argued that "whoever controls the Temple Mount has rights over the land of Israel."[2] For this reason these devotees of the Temple are prepared to do battle with the Muslims (who are in possession) and, if necessary, to destroy the Muslim holy sites to make way for the building of the Third Temple.[3] At a minimum, they demand the right to pray on this sacred soil.

---

[1] Yossi Klein Halevi, "The Battle for the Temple Mount," *Jerusalem Report*, October 3, 1996, p. 18.

[2] Cited in Eliezer Don-Yehiya "The Book and the Sword: The Nationalist Yeshivot and Political Radicalism in Israel," in Martin E. Marty and R. Scott Appleby, eds., *Accounting for Fundamentalisms: The Dynamic Character of Movements*, (Chicago: University of Chicago Press, 1994), pp. 264, 280. Other studies of the Temple Mount Faithful include Robert I. Friedman, *Zealots for Zion: Inside Israel's West Bank Movement* (New York: Random House, 1992), pp. 123–152. See also Roger Friedland and Richard Hecht, "The Politics of Sacred Space: Jerusalem's Temple Mount/*al-haram al-sharif*," in Jamie Scott and Paul Simpson-Housley, eds., *Sacred Spaces and Profane Spaces: Essays in the Geographies of Judaism, Christianity, and Islam*, (New York: Greenwood Press, 1991), pp. 21–22; Ehud Sprinzak, *The Ascendance of Israel's Radical Right* (New York: Oxford University Press, 1991), pp. 279–281.

[3] Some have urged that the mosques not be torn down but be moved instead. Thus, Yehuda Etzion once urged that, "every stone must be marked and labeled, and then moved. It should be moved to Mecca. That is the natural place for it. Here it is the wrong building in the wrong place"; Julian Borger, "When this Holy Beast Finally Goes Up in Flames, Pray to God There'll be no Millennium Mayhem," *Observer* (London), July 6, 1997, p. 5.

For a detailed analysis of the intellectual and theological underpinnings of the underground movement that plotted to destroy the mosques on the Temple Mount, including the role of Yehuda Etzion, see Sprinzak, *The Ascendance of Israel's Radical Right*, pp. 251–288. See also Scott and Simpson-Housley, *Sacred Spaces and Profane Spaces*.

The problem is relatively recent as the Temple Mount has not been in Jewish hands since the first century C.E. Traditionally, orthodox rabbis have banned Jews from entering the Temple Mount for fear of accidentally entering the site of the "Holy of Holies," which only the High Priest was allowed to enter once a year (the ban was restated by Sephardic chief rabbi Eliahu Bakshi-Doron as recently as June 1997).[4] Indeed, after the 1967 War, Israel's chief rabbis (one Ashkenazic and one Sephardic) issued a joint statement that forbade Jews from access to any part of the Temple Mount. This was followed days later by a similar decision of the Chief Rabbinate Council, and weeks later by the same announcement signed by up to 100 other leading rabbis.[5]

Since the exact site of this area is today uncertain, Jews were forbidden to enter the Temple Mount in its entirety for fear of accidental desecration.[6] The rest of the Temple area, according to Jewish law, can be entered only after special purification requiring the slaughtering, burning, and sprinkling of the ashes of a red heifer.[7] The laws of the red heifer are so complex that Maimonides ruled that only nine heifers existed until the destruction of the Second Temple, and that the tenth would be prepared only by the Messiah himself. To make matters even more complicated, the priest involved in the preparation of the ashes must already be ritually pure. Moreover, there are varying kinds of ritual impurity—such as that deriving from contact with a corpse—and Jewish law treats each differently as regards different areas of the Temple Mount.

Religious Jews therefore believe the restoration of the Temple[8] and the re-establishment of prayer on the Temple Mount should be left to Messianic times. Although all Orthodox rabbis perceive the rebuilding of the Temple as the culminating act of the redemption process, most consider that no particular

---

[4] Haim Shapiro, "Bakshi-Doron slams Temple Mount prayer," *Jerusalem Post*, June 9, 1997, p. 3. In a later statement urging restraint, Bakshi-Doron said that "by announcing that we are forbidden to go on the Temple Mount, we are proving that we are owners of this holy site." "Israeli Rabbis call for Jews not to pray at holy site," *Agence France Press*, August 4, 1997.

[5] See Yoel Cohen, "The Chief Rabbinate and the Temple Mount Question," paper presented at the Twelfth World Congress of Jewish Studies, Jerusalem, July–August 1997.

[6] Martin Gilbert relates that during the long drought of 1902, the Muslim community in desperation asked the Jewish leadership to try its hand at praying for rain on the Temple Mount. Conscious of the rabbinic injunction against entering the Temple grounds, the Jews asked instead for permission to pray at Mount Zion. Martin Gilbert, *Jerusalem in the Twentieth Century* (New York: John Wiley & Sons, 1996), p. 21.

[7] So far no red heifer has been found. But see text below, p. 56.

[8] One fascinating footnote to all this is the financial support that some Christian evangelicals—who believe the early rebuilding of the Third Temple will hasten the second coming of Christ—have given to the Jerusalem Temple Foundation for Temple Mount activities. See Michael and Barbara Ledeen, "The Temple Mount Plot: What do Christian and Jewish fundamentalists have in common," *New Republic*, June 18, 1984, p. 20. See also the description of such "Christian Zionists" in Robert Friedman, "Terror on Sacred Ground," *Mother Jones*, August/September 1987, p. 37.

individual or group will build the Temple and that it may be done only by the will of the entire Jewish people. The established Orthodox consensus is that conditions at present are not ripe for the building of the Third Temple.[9]

This consensus began to disintegrate because the nationalist ideologies found Muslim control (albeit *de facto*) of a Jewish holy site unsettling. As early as 1962, Rabbi Shlomo Goren, for example, told a conference on Jewish law that "if the Old City was ever captured, Jews would have an obligation to build the Temple." A month after the 1967 war, Goren (who as chief Army chaplain, was the first rabbi to reach the Western Wall after the 1967 war), reportedly told a group of reservist military rabbis that the mosques should be destroyed.[10] But then–Defense Minister Moshe Dayan intervened having already determined that the Temple Mount should be for Arabs, and the Western Wall for Jews.

In 1976, Goren prepared a halachic ruling allowing Jews to enter parts of the Temple Mount. The ruling was based on Goren's investigations into the geography of the Temple Mount site, which determined that the Holy of Holies was definitely within the Dome of the Rock; therefore Jewish law would permit access to the entry to the southern end of the Temple Mount (the area around the al-Aqsa Mosque).[11] Indeed, Goren has urged the building of a synagogue on the Mount itself.[12]

The number of Orthodox Jews interested in praying on the Temple Mount has increased considerably. Even those who would not enter the Temple Mount no longer view those concerned with Temple rituals and Temple prayer as fringe groups marginal to the religious world. For example, retired Supreme Court Justice Menachem Elon, in a public speech in June 1995, argued that the

---

[9] See Moshe Kohn, "Speedily in Our Time," *Jerusalem Post Magazine*, December 22, 1989, p. 6.

[10] "The military censor banned publication of the chief military rabbi's words, and in later years, Goren even gave out a veiled threat to sue a journalist who wanted to publish it. Goren, who personally participated in the battle for the capture of the Temple Mount was, in his own words, entranced—seeing the event as part of the Divine redemption." Yoel Cohen, "The Chief Rabbinate and the Temple Mount Question."

[11] Goren held off publishing the ruling, perhaps in deference to the Chief Rabbinate, which took the traditional position that entering the Temple Mount is forbidden. Goren's views became well known, however, and in 1988 he published a letter he had written some years earlier to the then-head of the Knesset Interior committee, Dov Shilansky, who had requested his views on the halachic parameters of a visit by Israeli members of Knesset. See Rabbi Shlomo Goren, "The Obligation to Enter the Temple Mount," *Tzfia*, no. 3 (1988), pp. 5–8 (Hebrew), and *Meshiv Milchama: Responsa on Issues of Army, War, and Security,* book 4: *Sefer Har HaBayit* (Jerusalem: Hotsa 'at 'ha-Idra rabah', 1992) (Hebrew).

[12] This concern to maintain a Jewish presence on *Har HaBayit* led former Sephardic chief rabbi Mordechai Eliahu to propose "the construction of a synagogue to the northern area of the Temple Mount. The synagogue's structure would comprise a single entrance from the northern tip of the Mount, and there would be no exit way onto the Mount, but rather, a sheer glass wall enabling the worshipers to look out onto the Mount." See Yoel Cohen, "The Chief Rabbinate and the Temple Mount Question," p. 5.

government has no right to prevent prayer on the Temple Mount on the part of religious Jews who follow rabbis who believe it to be permitted.[13]

Not all religious Jews view these events in a positive light. The *haredi* (ultra-orthodox) public is hostile to groups like the Temple Mount Faithful, viewing the motivation of the latter as nationalist not religious. For its part, the nonreligious public remains largely indifferent.[14] Yet the issue continues to resonate. In May 1997, sixty rabbis from the West Bank who form the Council of Rabbis for Judea and Samaria broke ranks with the religious establishment and urged their adherents to attempt to ascend Har HaBayit to pray (whether for religious reasons or generally to cause a confrontation is unclear). The rabbis claimed that "We now have enough data to ascend without making a mistake. . . . We are waiting for the redemption and the reconstruction of the Temple, which must begin quickly in our day."[15]

And the birth in 1997 at Kfar Hassidim, near Haifa, of a calf that approximated the religious criteria for the red heifer created religious excitement among many orthodox.[16] According to some, its discovery would enable the purificiation rituals that are a prerequisite for the construction of the Third Temple. One reporter called the calf "a bomb walking on four legs."[17] Most rabbinical authorities, however, agreed that there were too many religious problems involved in the use of a red heifer—including the fact that only a priest in a state of ritual purity can sacrifice it—for such a discovery to have any practical effect.[18]

Religious issues connected to the holy places permeate Jerusalem. Organizations like the Temple Institute sponsor lectures and research that heighten awareness of the centrality of the Temple and the Temple Mount in Jewish thought and practice.

---

[13] See Amnon Ramon, *The Attitude of the State of Israel and the Jewish Public to the Temple Mount (1967–1996)* (Jerusalem: Jerusalem Institute of Israel Studies, 1997), pp. 26–27 (Hebrew).

[14] Ibid., pp. 23–24.

[15] See "Jews reportedly urged to pray near mosque," *Washington Times*, May 28, 1997, p. A11. See also Julian Borger, "When this Holy Beast Finally Goes Up in Flames. . .," p. 5.

[16] Ethan Bronner, "Heifer's appearance in Israel stirs hopes, apocalyptic fears," *Boston Globe*, April 6, 1997, p. A1; Kendall Hamilton, "The Strange Case of Israel's Red Heifer," *Newsweek*, May 19, 1997, p. 16; and, Serge Schmemann, "A Red Heifer, or Not? Rabbi Wonders," *New York Times*, June 14, 1997, p. 4.

[17] David Landau, "The Red Heifer: it is not funny." *Ha'aretz,* March 26, 1997 p. 1 (Hebrew). A Christian evangelical cattle breeder in Georgia has recently claimed to have bred a ritually appropriate heifer. See also Steve Levin, "Red Heifer Quest Brings Together Jews, Christians," *Pittsburgh Gazette*, May 28, 1997, p. A1; and "Apocalypse Cow," *New York Times*, March 30, 1997, p. 17.

[18] As this book went to press the authors learned that the Kfar Hassidim heifer was a "false sighting": The animal's tail was turning white. Tom Segev, "The heifer that was a lemon." *Ha'aretz,* January 16, 1998, p. 8 (English edition).

One *yeshiva* (rabbinical seminary), Ateret Cohanim, or the "Priestly Crown," was situated in the Muslim Quarter specifically to study the laws pertaining to the operation of the Temple. In the early 1980s, Ateret Cohanim founded a subsidiary, the Jerusalem Reclamation Project, to purchase homes in the Muslim and Christian quarters for Jewish housing.[19] At least thirty buildings in the Old City have been purchased by Jews, and the yeshiva itself is based in a building in the Muslim quarter that housed a yeshiva before 1948.[20]

Much of this activity has been fueled by contributions from American philanthropists including Irving Moskowitz, a retired Miami doctor.[21] Moskowitz himself purchased the land in the Ras al-Amud section of eastern Jerusalem that is the site of the controversial Jewish housing complex.[22] After international protest and the opposition of Prime Minister Netanyahu, the settlers vacated the premises, leaving ten seminary students to "maintain" the house and building site.[23]

In early February 1998, however, the Interior Ministry gave permission to build, this time including Arab housing as well. The prime minister's office continues to oppose this particular expansion as Ras al-Amud is already an Arab neighborhood. While this version of Ras al-Amud expansion is blocked for the moment, there can be little doubt that the logic of continued expansion of Jewish settlement in built-up areas of eastern Jerusalem is a certain recipe for communal conflict.[24]

---

[19] Robert Friedman, *Zealots for Zion*, pp. 96–104; see also Robert Friedman, "The Redemption of Arab Jerusalem: Is American Money Financing Israeli Land Purchases in the Muslim Quarter?," *Washington Post*, January 10, 1988.

[20] In 1990, during Easter week, Ateret Cohanim extended its range of activities into the Christian quarter when its members moved into St. John's Hospice near the Church of the Holy Sepulchre. Although the exact facts remain in dispute, it appears that the building was owned by the Greek Orthodox Church, which leased it for decades to an Armenian named Martyos Matossian. In 1989, Matossian in turn sublet it to a Panamanian front for Ateret Cohanim. The Greeks protested and, in the resulting riots, the Greek Orthodox patriarch was thrown to the ground and severely injured. The matter ended up in prolonged litigation, and tension between the Christian and Jewish communities grew markedly. See Robert Friedman, *Zealots for Zion*, pp. 96–104.

[21] For more on Moskowitz and his land purchase activity, see Serge Schmemann with James Brooke, "U.S. Doctor's Donations Fuel Mideast Storms," *New York Times*, September 29, 1997, p. 1; Marilyn Henry, "Who is Moskowitz?" *Jerusalem Post*, August 1, 1997, p. 8; and Lawrence Cohler-Esses, "A Tale of Two Cities," *Jewish Week*, September 26, 1997, p. 1.

[22] Leslie Susser, "The Mayor and the Millionaire," *Jerusalem Report*, October 16, 1997, pp. 14–20; Jean-Luc Renaudie, "Netanyahu fails to pursuade US bankroller of settlers to back down," *Agence France Presse*, September 16, 1997.

[23] "Ras al-Amud Crisis Defused," *Facts on File*, October 23, 1997; Laurie Copans, "Palestinian files claim to disputed eastern Jerusalem house," *Agence France Presse*, September 22, 1997.

[24] See "Ministry Okays Jewish Housing in Ras al-Amud," *Jerusalem Post*, February 4, 1998, p. 1; Elli Wohlgelernter, "Government Vows to Block Building in Ras al-Amud," *Jerusalem Post*, February 5, 1998, p. 1; Joel Greenberg, "Israeli Officials Split Over Plan to Settle Jews in East Jerusalem," *New York Times*, February 5, 1998, p. A5.

VII

Jerusalem and the Holy Places

More than sixty proposals for the solution of the Jerusalem problem, beginning with the Sykes–Picot Agreement of 1916, are described in *Whither Jerusalem?* (1995).[1] These proposals suggest that Jerusalem remain either undivided under Israeli sovereignty, or physically undivided but politically separated under dual or shared Israeli and Palestinian sovereignty.

Every proposal recommends guarantees for the security of the holy places, for freedom of worship and access, for rights of pilgrims, and for administration of the holy places by the various religious organizations themselves. Some proposals suggest that international committees be formed to supervise the Christian holy places and that the United Nations appoint a kind of high commissioner who could supervise and act as arbitrator in disputes over the holy places.

It is noteworthy that whatever apprehensions may exist about future conflict between Arabs and Jews in the Temple Mount/Haram area, they are not present with the Christians and their shrines. But of course the Christian communities, taken as a whole, are not at the center of the nationalistic struggle over this country and capital. The disputes of Christians and Jews over the holy places are concerned with issues of religious freedom and religious autonomy. The disputes between Muslims and Jews are additionally wrapped up in political issues of sovereignty and land.

PAST PROPOSALS FOR THE FUTURE OF JERUSALEM

The first proposal, suggesting that Jerusalem should remain undivided under Israeli sovereignty, is favored overwhelmingly by the Israeli people and by their political parties, including Labor and Likud. Those who make this proposal usually recommend that some "arrangement" be made to meet the needs of political self-representation on the part of Arab Jerusalemites. That "arrangement" varies from proposal to proposal but usually includes schemes for a mixed municipal council or Arab Jerusalem boroughs—all under overarching Israeli government authority. Many of these plans recognize some special arrangement for the Muslim holy places in any final settlement. As far back as

---

[1] Moshe Hirsch, Deborah Housen-Couriel, and Ruth Lapidoth, eds., *Whither Jerusalem? Proposals and Positions Concerning the Future of Jerusalem* (Boston: Martinus Nijhoff, 1995).

July 1968, Shlomo Hillel, then of the Foreign Ministry, pointed out that any settlement on Jerusalem "will contain steps which will satisfy the need of the Muslims for status—extraterritorial standing and the right to raise flags."[2]

There is little doubt that Israel would like to get Palestinian and Jordanian consent to some "arrangement" for Jerusalem, as described above. This is reinforced by a recent perceptive article by Menachem Klein, "The Islamic Holy Places as a Political Bargaining Card (1993–1995)."[3] Klein suggests that in negotiations affecting the current peace process, Israel effectively gained Jordanian acquiescence to Israeli sovereignty over eastern Jerusalem in exchange for Israeli recognition of Jordan's authority over the Haram al-Sharif and its mosques. This exchange, asserts Klein, forced PLO chairman Yasir Arafat to mobilize international Arab condemnation of Jordan for recognizing Israeli sovereignty over eastern Jerusalem. Pressure was then put on Jordan to agree that should eastern Jerusalem becomes a Palestinian capital, Jordan will recognize Palestinian authority over the Haram.

What is clear from Klein's argument is that the current peace process has put Israel squarely in the middle of the tensions between Jordan and the Palestinians, certainly affecting the future of eastern Jerusalem and its Muslim holy places.

The second proposal—that Jerusalem should be physically undivided but politically separated under dual or shared Israeli and Palestinian sovereignty—is favored by many who believe it is the one solution that is both morally symmetrical and, ultimately, politically acceptable. Dual sovereignty seems to be the current position of the Palestinian Authority.

Under the dual sovereignty proposal, Arab and Jewish municipalities would exist side by side, each of which would exercise administrative, economic, and policymaking authority. Legal disputes and issues of jurisdiction would be decided by a standing Israeli–Palestinian committee on Jerusalem.

The Old City and particularly its neighborhoods and its shrines, all lying cheek by jowl, would pose a problem for the dual sovereignty proposal. The problem is usually met by subproposals for extending Jewish sovereignty to the Jewish Quarter, Arab sovereignty to the Muslim Quarter, and offering Christians the option of choosing either Arab or Jewish sovereignty.

Critics of the dual sovereignty proposal fault it for blurring the lines of governing authority in Jerusalem and for a lack of political realism. As one of us has written in another context,

> Even with the best will in the world, dual sovereignty won't work, in part for reasons of public administration. Shared sovereignty does not mean shared authority. Rather, as Teddy Kollek insightfully points out, it ends up meaning 'two competing authorities and ultimately two sets of laws, two rates of customs and taxation, two police forces.' . . . In

---

[2] Terrence Prittie, *Whose Jerusalem?* (London: Frederick Muller Ltd., 1981), p. 186.

[3] Menachem Klein, "The Islamic Holy Places as a Political Bargaining Card (1993–1995)," *Catholic University Law Review* 45 (1996), p. 745.

the end, because dual sovereignty is no more than a mirage, demands for such solutions will ineluctably collapse, in practice, into some variant of a divided city. And very likely a return to a walled city as well.[4]

To the vast majority of Israelis the slogan "undivided Jerusalem" means that the whole city will never again be divided physically or politically. Most Israelis from across the political spectrum see Jerusalem as the symbol of a revived Jewish people in its sovereign state, and the thought of ceding the sovereignty of some part of Jerusalem to an Arab government is simply anathema to them.

PROPOSALS FOR THE FUTURE OF THE HOLY PLACES

Administrative arrangements for the future of the holy places are a subset of proposals for the future of Jerusalem. They tend to be ambiguous in at least one respect; it is often unclear to what extent they are designed to deal with the problem of administering scattered religious sites throughout Jerusalem and to what extent they are, in fact, proposed arrangements for the "Old City"—the site of so many of the holy places. The Israelis invariably intend the former, yet many of the proposals would likely encompass the latter.

One can take at least three approaches to the problem of the holy places. One approach is to transfer power (or control) over the holy places to an interfaith committee[5] consisting of representatives of the various "stakeholders," specifically the Christian churches, Muslim groups, and of course the Jewish community. Indeed, Article 14 of the League of Nations Mandate called for creation of a "special commission" to be "appointed by the Mandatory to study and define the rights and claims in connection with the holy places and the rights and claims relating to the different religious communities of Palestine."[6] The 1948 debates in the UN Trusteeship Council over the legislative council to be set up in the so called *corpus separatum* underscore this point. The French proposal called for a Council of Thirty: ten Jews, ten Muslims, and ten Christians.[7] In recent years, Walid Khalidi urged this approach with his proposals for an "interfaith council" to govern the holy places.[8] In December 1996, King Hussein

[4] Marshall J. Breger, "Jerusalem, Now and Then; The New Battle for Jerusalem," *Middle East Quarterly* (December 1994), pp. 32–33.

[5] See Michael Parks, "Israel Suggests Shared Control of Holy Sites," *Los Angeles Times*, July 20, 1994, p. A1, for a report that Israeli diplomats have raised this notion; David Horowitz, "Holy Sites May Go to Impartial Outside Control," *Irish Times*, July 13, 1994, p. 9.

[6] Mandate for Palestine, in Lapidoth and Hirsch, in Ruth Lapidoth and Moshe Hirsch, eds., *The Arab–Israel Conflict and its Resolution: Selected Documents* (Boston: Martinus Nijhoff Publishers, 1991), p. 28. This commission was never created due in large measure to disputes between the various religious bodies as to its composition.

[7] Larry Kletter, "The Sovereignty of Jerusalem in International Law," *Columbia Journal of Transnational Law* 20 (1981), pp. 319, 337.

[8] Walid Khalidi, "Thinking the Unthinkable: A Sovereign Palestinian State," *Foreign Affairs* 56,

invited leaders of all monotheistic religious faiths to Amman to discuss religious issues related to Jerusalem.[9] The Israeli government response was favorable, if guarded.

A second approach is to devolve power to committees of the relevant religious confessions. International lawyer Elihu Lauterpacht urged such a resolution in his 1968 study of the status of the holy places.[10] Thus, a Muslim committee would govern the Muslim holy sites and a Christian committee would govern the Christian holy sites; presumably the Israeli political system could handle the problem of the Jewish holy sites without any international approbation. This approach has been called "functional internationalization."[11] Under this concept the holy places are not placed under the sovereignty of an international entity but rather under the command of the religious groups concerned with each site.[12]

Indeed, the historical record indicates that Israel, while rejecting international interference with the secular political status of Jerusalem, has contemplated some form of "functional" autonomy or a measure of international supervision over the holy places as part of a comprehensive settlement.[13] Abba Eban said as much to the United Nations in discussions preceding Israel's admission in 1949;[14] in 1967

---

no. 4 (July 1978), pp. 695–713. Analagous approaches are contained in Mosche Hirsch, Deborah Housen-Couriel, and Ruth Lapidoth, *Whither Jerusalem,?* as follows: the United Nations Special Committee on Palestine, submitted to the General Assembly on August 31, 1947 (p. 34); Prof. Benjamin Akzin (p. 47); Amb. James George (p. 73); Shmuel Berkovitz (p. 74); and Justice Haim Cohn (p. 93).

[9] See "Jordan Welcomes Israeli Response to Initiative on Jerusalem," *Deutsche Presse-Agentor*, December 29, 1996.

[10] Elihu Lauterpacht, *Jerusalem and the Holy Places* (London: Anglo–Israel Association, 1968), pp. 58–59.

[11] This approach would restrict international interests to the protection of the holy places while delegating secular administration to the states actually exercising control. Shlomo Slonim, "United States Policy on Jerusalem," *Catholic University Law Review* 45 (1996), p. 820; see also Rüdiger Wolfram, "Internationalization," in Rudolf Bernhardt, ed., *Encyclopedia of Public International Law* 2 (New York: Elsevier, 1995), pp. 1395–1398, for a discussion of the concept of functional internationalization.

[12] Mark Gruhin, "Jerusalem: Legal and Political Dimensions in a Search for Peace," *Case Western Reserve Journal of International Law* 12 (1980), p. 209; see also Larry Kletter, "The Sovereignty of Jerusalem in International Law," *Columbia Journal of Transnational Law* 20 (1981), p. 356.

[13] Yehuda Z. Blum, *The Juridical Status of Jerusalem* (Jerusalem: Hebrew University of Jerusalem, 1974), p. 26. Israel supported a Swedish proposal for functional autonomy in 1950 that specifically called for a UN commissioner to supervise access to and protection of the holy places. The Jordanians rejected the Swedish proposal as an infringement on their sovereignty. Ibid., p. 27. See also Elihu Lauterpacht, *Jerusalem and the Holy Places*, p. 30.

[14] Eban, however, restricted international involvement "so that it would be concerned only with the protection of the holy places and not with any purely secular aspects of life and government." Yehuda Z. Blum, *The Juridical Status of Jerusalem*, p. 27. Extracts of the statement can be found in Lapidoth and Hirsch, *The Arab–Israel Conflict*, p. 43. Four years later, Foreign Minister Moshe

in a letter addressed to the Secretary General of the UN; and in 1969 in a speech to the General Assembly.[15]

This devolution is easier said than done. First, there is the obvious question of the composition of each governing council. History has made clear how difficult it will be for each confessional community to cooperate in administring the holy sites. Indeed, the best way for this problem to be resolved from Israel's perspective may be for Israel to tell both Muslims and Christians that Israel will accept any arrangement for each religion that all the parts of that religious community agree to; they would likely come back asking Israel to impose a solution.

Second, many questions regarding the areas of religious council control remain. One commentator has suggested that "each religious site would be free from municipal or national tax and vested with a qualified diplomatic status. Preservation, maintenance, and protection of the holy places would be issues open to discussion."[16] The devil, of course, is in the details: Does the religious council control include any police powers or fines for littering? prosecutions for theft or murder? and how about extradition of suspects or criminals for prosecution in Israeli (or even Palestinian) courts?[17]

One model for this approach might be found in the governance of the Mt. Athos peninsula in Greece. Mt. Athos is a wooded peninsula in Northern Greece about thirty-five miles long and from two to five miles wide.[18] It is home to more than twenty orthodox monasteries and more than 1,500 monks.[19] It is under

---

Sharett reaffirmed this view in the Knesset, drawing the distinction between "the status of Jerusalem as a city and capital and the status of the holy places." Ibid., p. 28. A text of the full statement can be found in Lapidoth and Hirsch, *The Arab–Israel Conflict*, p. 74.

[15] As Blum clearly summarizes, even after the June 1967 War, Israel remained faithful to the policy that the sacred shrines located in and around Jerusalem should be made the responsibility of those who have traditionally held them sacred. Yehuda Blum, *The Juridical Status of Jerusalem,* pp. 30–31.

[16] Ibid. See also Mark Gruhin,"Jerusalem: Legal and Political Dimensions in a Search for Peace," p. 209.

[17] We should remember that when the former *mufti* was wanted by the British for inciting the "Arab riots" during the late 1930s, he effectively claimed "sanctuary" on the Haram, hiding there while the British hesitated to enter the Haram to arrest him, for fear of Arab reaction. After Palestinian extremists murdered the district commissioner of Galilee, the *mufti*, fearing that Muslim troops from India would be brought in to arrest him, climbed down the walls of the Haram and escaped to Lebanon. Philip Mattar, *The Mufti of Jerusalem: Al-Hajj Amin al-Husayni and the Palestinian National Movement* (New York: Columbia University Press, 1988), pp. 82–83.

[18] Mt. Athos, unlike Israel, was never a sovereign state. It was part of the *territorium* first of the Byzantine and then of the Ottoman Empire. Charalambos K. Papastathis, "The Status of Mount Athos in Hellenic Public Law," in Anthony-Emil N. Tachraos, ed., *Mount Athos and the European Community* (Thessalonika: Institute for Balkan Studies, 1993), p. 56.

[19] See John Julius Norwich and Reresby Sitwell, *Mount Athos* (New York: Harper & Row, 1966); see also Philip Sherrard, *Athos: the Holy Mountain* (Woodstock, N.Y.: Overlook Press, 1982).

formal Greek sovereignty, but "in accordance with its ancient privileged status," the Greek constitution grants Mt. Athos self-government under a "Holy Community," or religious council, which consists of representatives of the twenty monasteries, and an Epistasia, vested with executive power and composed of four members of the "Holy Community."[20] This arrangement is based on a charter drawn up in 1924 by the Athonite community, the political aspects of which the Greek government subsequently ratified, while the Greek Orthodox Patriachate in Istanbul ratified its "spiritual" aspects.[21]

Whereas the Greek state remains "exclusively responsible for safeguarding public order and security," the charter allows Mt. Athos to have its own police force, misdemeanor courts, and taxation system within the rubric of the Greek state. They are free from taxation and exempt from most customs and import duties.[22] To enter the peninsula, visitors must get special permits, which are provided only upon receipt of letters of recommendation from a foreign embassy.[23] Serious crimes are sent to the civil courts in Salonika. In addition, the Epistasia has specific enforcement powers.[24] At the same time, Mt. Athos is not fully cut off from the Greek state. Indeed a civil governor resides in Karyes, the capital. He is not the chief administrator—the Epistasia performs the peninsula's administrative functions—rather he serves as a representative of the Greek government who can void Athonian legislation as beyond the authority of the charter and against the "holy privileges" of Mt. Athos.[25]

---

[20] Article 105 of The Greek Constitution of 1975 is most easily accessible as an appendix in Charalambos K. Papastathis, "The Hellenic Republic and the Prevailing Religion," *Brigham Young University Law Review* 815 (1996), p. 851. See also John Julius Norwich and Reresby Sitwell, *Mount Athos*, pp. 87-90.

[21] These institutional arrangements are described in Philip Sherrard, *Athos: the Mountain of Silence* (London: Oxford University Press, 1960), pp. 22–26.

[22] A list of these exemptions can be found in Charalambos K. Papastathis, "State Financial Support for the Church in Greece," *Church and State in Europe* (Milan: Giuffrè Editore, 1992), pp. 15–16.

[23] Friends of Mt. Athos, *Newsletter*, No. 4 (1997).

[24] Consider Philip Sherrard's description of the Epistasia:

> The executive or Epistasia is responsible for the cleanliness and the lighting of the streets of Karyes, and for the general sanitation of the village; it regulates food prices, prohibits songs, games, musical instruments, smoking, and horseback riding in the streets. It forbids, too, the opening of shops during vespers, Sundays, and feast-days, and the sale of meat and non-ascetic foods on Wednesday and Fridays and other fast-days; it may expel the drunken, the unemployed and the disorderly from the community; it is, finally, the channel through which inter-monastic disputes may be submitted to the assembly. To assist it in its functions, the Epistasia has at its disposal a local guard, and may also call upon the civil police for assistance.

Philip Sherrard, *Athos: The Holy Mountain*, p. 72.

[25] If a dispute should arise between the Governor and the holy community, the Governor seeks the guidance of the Minister of Foreign Affairs.

Various international treaties have provided guarantees for Mt. Athos's autonomy.[26] In the Treaty of Berlin, the European powers provided guarantees for the autonomy of Mt. Athos that were reiterated in the Treaty of Sévrès (1920), which acknowledged Greek sovereignty on Mt. Athos and asserted the obligation of Greece "to recognize and preserve the traditional rights and liberties enjoyed by the non-Greek monastic communities on Mt. Athos."[27] This language was incorporated into the Treaty of Lausanne—the 1923 peace treaty between Turkey and Greece[28]—and to this extent the Greek constitution both recognizes and implements these international obligations. Further, in the agreement providing for the accession of Greece to the European Community in 1979, the European Economic Community agreed that the special status of Mt. Athos will be "taken into account in the application and subsequent preparation of provisions of community law, in particular in relation to customs franchise privileges, tax exemptions, and the right of establishment."[29]

The present political organization on Athos is well-secured in that it is based on a charter that cannot be modified by the Greek parliament. Changes must be approved first by the Holy Community on Athos, then by the Ecumenical patriarch in Constantinople, and finally by the Greek parliament in Athens.[30] The Greek parliament, moreover, can only ratify a draft presented to it; it cannot on its own propose emendations.

The most recent threat to the political independence of Athos has come from the Church, not the state. In 1994, the patriarch in Constantinople sent a delegation of three bishops to preside over a session of the Holy Community. The majority of the council rejected such interference and boycotted the session, thus allowing the remaining members to depose an abbot and representatives of the three monasteries. In response, the boycotting "majority" declared themselves "persecuted" by the Patriarchate and announced that, because of the Patriarchate's efforts to intervene in local Athonian affairs, relations with

---

[26] Charalambos K. Papastathis, "The Status of Mount Athos in Hellenic Public Law," pp. 55–75. See Treaty of Berlin, Art. 62, 83 Parl. Papers 690–705 (July 13, 1878). The Treaty of Sévrès specifically made reference to the Treaty of Berlin's protection of the rights and liberties of the monastic communities in Article 62. See Treaty of Sévrès, Art. 13, 1920 Gr.Brit.T.S. No. 11 (Cmd. 961), in *American Journal of International Law* 15 (New York: Oxford University Press, 1921), pp. 179–295.

[27] Ibid. See generally, Charalambos K. Papastathis,"The Nationality of the Mount Athos Monks of non-Greek Origin," *Balkan Studies* 8 (1967), pp. 75–86.

[28] Treaty with Turkey and other Instruments Signed at Lausanne, Art. 16, July 24, 1923, 28 UNTS 12, in *American Journal of International Law* 18 Supp. (Concord, N.H.: Rumford Press, 1924), pp. 1–115.

[29] *Official Journal of the European Communities* L 291, vol. 22 (November 19, 1979), p. 186.

[30] Article 105 of the Greek Constitution. The situation on Mt. Athos is well-reviewed by Silvio Ferrari, "The Religious Significance of Jerusalem in the Middle East Peace Process: Some Legal Implications," *Catholic University of America Law Review* 45 (1996), pp. 737–738.

Constantinople were "severely strained."[31] In contrast, when the socialist government of Greece appropriated 350,000 acres of church land to distribute to farm cooperatives, it specifically exempted Mt. Athos from the decree.[32]

A third approach to the problem of the holy places would be to leave the matter to various international guarantees such as the UNESCO and Hague Conventions discussed earlier.[33] Israel already subscribes to many of these guarantees and thus reaffirmation would be a relatively simple act that could satisfy both the Israeli need for sovereignty and the religious communities' need for some indication of international involvement. Alternatively, Israel may choose to bind itself on these matters unilaterally,[34] forgoing the difficulties of hammering out a multilateral or bilateral agreement. Indeed, some commentators have suggested that existing Israeli statements in international forums regarding Israel's commitment to protect the holy places and freedom of access to them already have created some form of customary obligation under international law.[35]

In recent months there has been within Israel a veritable farrago of "final status" scenarios that have, in some instances, encompassed concrete proposals for the holy places. These have included, among others, the summer 1995 discussions between Palestinian and Israeli academics including Oslo "architect" Yair Hirschfield;[36] the Beilin–Abu Mazen "non-paper" of November 1995;[37] and the Beilin–Eitan proposal of January 1997.[38]

---

[31] This "crisis" between Church and Church is described in Leonard Doyle, "Mt. Athos Under Siege: Monks in Greek Island at Odds with Religious Leaders, Government," *San Francisco Examiner*, April 3, 1994, p. A15; Paul Anast, "Monastic State Fights Besieging Bishops," *Daily Telegraph* (London), March 4, 1994, p. 10; Sir Steven Runciman et al., "Schism and Anger on Mount Athos," Letter to *The Times* (London), March 3, 1994.

[32] "Legislation Takes Church Lands," *Facts on File World News Digest*, May 8, 1987, p. 337A3.

[33] See text above, pp. 21–22, and accompanying notes.

[34] See *Nuclear Tests* [Australia. v. France], ICJ Reports 1974, pp. 267–270, holding that France was legally bound by unilateral promises to refrain from nuclear testing in the Pacific, even absent reliance by other states. See also Geoffrey R. Watson, "The Death of Treaty," *Ohio Law Journal* 55 (1994), pp. 781, 794–814, critiquing *Nuclear Tests* and discussing "international promissory estoppel."

[35] This seems to be the view of Enrico Molinaro in "Israel's Position on Jerusalem and International Norms for the Holy Places," *Jerusalem Letter* 342, Jerusalem Center for Public Affairs (September 6, 1996).

[36] Regarding the holy places, Hirschfield states: "The Old City itself would not be under anyone's sovereignty, but in effect the sovereignty would be Israeli—unrecognized by the Palestinians— [since it would be] under the control of the Jerusalem municipality. That is to say, only Israeli police would be there and no other police. . . . The Palestinian capital would be in Abu Dis, which is outside the muncipal borders of Jerusalem." Evelyn Gordon, "Hirschfield: Temple Mount Would Have Gone to Palestinians if Peres Had Won," *Jerusalem Post*, July 31, 1996, p. 2.

[37] See text above, p. 29 and note 15.

[38] See Serge Schmemann, "Likud and Labor Legislators Draft Bipartisan Peace Plan," *New York Times*, January 26, 1997, p. 6.

The most widely discussed of these, the Beilin–Abu Mazen non-paper, while never officially released, has been leaked in innumerable press reports. As regards Jerusalem and the holy places it would

• establish a Palestinian capital in Abu Dis (an Arab village just outside Jerusalem), where a future Palestinian parliament might be situated. Abu Dis would be renamed al-Quds (Arabic for Jerusalem);

• leave the Temple Mount as is, under *de facto* Palestinian control, while formally "suspending" Israeli sovereignty to reflect that reality. As a result, the Palestinian flag would be allowed to fly on the Mount;

• leave practical control over the entire city in Israeli hands; and

• incorporate the close-in West Bank Jewish city of Ma'aleh Adumim into Israel's capital.

Beilin and Abu Mazen apparently did not agree on the matter of *de jure* sovereignty for eastern Jerusalem (some say the Old City) and agreed to continue with practical control in Israeli hands, leaving the matter for later discussion.[39]

As a practical matter none of the holy places—including the Temple Mount—realistically raise issues of sovereignty as we understand it in the West; they are simply too small to exist even as postage stamp principalities. The Vatican, we must remember, is 109 acres with a population of 400, while the Haram is no more than 35 acres with only a negligible population, if any. The realistic options presented are some form of so-called extraterritoriality under a Pan-Islamic commission, formal recognition of autonomy under the waqf, or some form of autonomy reinforced by international guarantees as in the Mt. Athos model. Symbolism aside, any of these models is likely to be similar in their day-to-day operation.

---

[39] Regarding the Beilin–Abu Mazen "non-paper" Israeli member of Knesset Yossi Beilin, a principal negotiator in the Oslo talks, has suggested that Israel was prepared to recognize a Palestinian state, had the Palestinians "dropped demands to establish their capital in eastern Jerusalem. . . . [and] set up their capital in Abu Dis . . . [and] Israel would retain sovereignty over all Jerusalem, but the Arab neighborhoods in eastern Jerusalem would be granted wide-ranging autonomy." News Agencies, "Beilin: Israel Was Ready to Accept Palestinian State," *Jerusalem Post*, August 1, 1996, p. 12.

VIII

Ten Lessons to Be Learned

A review of the past history of Jerusalem and the holy places suggests a number of lessons that can be useful to both the day-to-day administration of the city's sacred space as well as the future negotiations over Jerusalem as envisioned in the Oslo Accords.

The *first lesson* recalls the famous dictum of Robert Frost, "Good fences make good neighbors." Never was this more true than in Jerusalem and its neighborhoods. Whatever peace Jerusalem has known in the past has come about because quarters, compounds, and neighborhoods were recognized and respected as belonging to a specific people, practicing their own particular lifestyle. For example, the recognized Jewish ultra-Orthodox quarter of Mea Shearim involves a distinctive and unalterable lifestyle. No one would think of opening a discotheque in Mea Shearim, but one could open a discotheque in East Talpiot, where few Orthodox are to be found. In this case, fences do not refer to tangible barriers—no "Berlin Walls" for Jerusalem—but rather understandings that evolve over time through common interest and consent that govern behavior between and among communities.

"Good fences" may be a valuable heuristic principle to meet the challenge of Jerusalem's diversity. This principle has important political implications. For example, notwithstanding their clear legal right to do so, one can question the historic wisdom of Jews to purchase or lease apartments and open Talmudic seminaries in the Muslim quarter of the Old City. Applying the "good fences" principle would mean that the Israeli government would not encourage Jews to locate in the Muslim quarter or to build in specifically Muslim neighborhoods, (just as the Israeli courts in 1968 prevented a Muslim, Mohammed Burkan, from purchasing his old house in the Jewish Quarter on grounds that property in the Jewish Quarter was restricted to Jews).[1] Parenthetically, it would mean that Jerusalem authorities would recognize the neighborhood claims of both *haredi* and secular Jews when approaching disputes such as those over the opening of Bar-Ilan Street on the sabbath.

Several years ago, the decision of a Jewish ultranationalist group, Ateret Cohanim, to lease a former Christian hospice, St. Johns, and move whole

---

[1] See HCJ 114/78, *Burkan v. Minister of Finance*, 32(2) PD 800 (1978). The case is excerpted in *Israel Yearbook on Human Rights* 20 (1990), p. 374, and is thoughtfully analyzed in David Kretzmer, *The Legal Status of Arabs in Israel* (Boulder, Colo.: Westview, 1990), pp. 77–85.

families into the heart of the Palestinian-populated Christian quarter of the Old City provoked riots throughout eastern Jerusalem. The Greek Orthodox Church, legal owner of the building, refused to tolerate the lease arrangement and found itself at odds with the Jewish group and with the Israeli government, whose officials were said to have funded and encouraged the Jewish group to locate in the Old City. Here, one could argue that the actions of Ateret Cohanim and government officials violated the principle of "good fences."[2]

The *second lesson* extends the "good fences" doctrine to Jerusalem's holy places. Whatever security and safety, tranquility, and decorum the holy places have known is due to the rules or "good fences" present in these places. When ambiguity about a holy place prevailed, when no one was sure who could worship where, when, and how—as often happened in the Church of the Holy Sepulcher and in the Western Wall/Temple Mount area—then conflict was sure to ensue.

The Israeli government over the years has been largely sensitive to this approach. It is understandable that Israel could not accept the Ottoman and British "status quo" as regards the Muslim holy sites, as doing so would have severely limited Jews' ability to worship freely at the Western Wall (as the debate during the Mandate made clear).[3] Nonetheless, the Israelis have been careful to allow the *waqf,* or Muslim charitable trust, effective control over the Haram except in the area of public order. At the same time, without reaffirming the status quo agreements covering worship at the Christian holy places, Israel has accepted the status quo in spirit, if not in letter.

Israeli courts have fashioned a useful distinction between private contemplation and public worship for Jews on the Temple Mount/Haram area. They have sustained this distinction by its use of the "public order" exception to practically limit Jewish prayer on the Haram. This distinction may be analytically unstable, however, and the Israeli government may be well advised to adopt the wisdom of the British formulation in the 1924 Order-in-Council that focused on the political rather than the legal rationale for resisting Jewish communal prayer on Har HaBayit. That is, in any event, the underlying premise of the "public order" exception. As a political matter, the issue could be raised as part of any overall "final" settlement where formulations that would accommodate all parties' religious sensibilities could be explored.

The *third lesson* undergirds the "good fences" principle. It suggests that, as regards the holy places at least, symbolic rhetoric often gets in the way of practical management. This is especially true as regards sovereignty, a concept that westerners imported into the Middle East. For centuries, the Ottoman administrative structure provided significant religious minorities with religious

---

[2] See Thomas A. Idinopulos, "Religious Turmoil in Zion," *Christian Century*, January 2–9, 1991, pp. 372–376.

[3] See text above, pp. 8–10 and accompanying notes.

and cultural autonomy through the millet system described earlier. Then, in the nineteenth century, citizens of western countries retained numerous special communal privileges under various capitulation agreements. For centuries, the Mamluk emirs ruled Egypt under the nominal suzerainty of the Sublime Porte in Constantinople. Indeed, until the centralizing efforts of the Young Turks in the last years of the empire, the sultan ruled largely through his annual claim of tribute in much of the Ottoman lands. For the rest of the year the local governor held sway.

It is not surprising, then, that the academic discipline most sensitive to problems of sovereignty—international law—understands the notion as encompassing a "bundle of rights" rather than an indivisible whole. In that regard some of Ruth Lapidoth's efforts to think through the implication of what she calls "functional sovereignty" and "suspended sovereignty" (and what others have called "functional internationalization") may be particularly useful.[4] This means focusing on specifics like police, sewage, building permits, public order, and sanctuary. Following that approach, Israel could usefully begin to explore the Mt. Athos model to consider the extent to which that modality might provide necessary autonomy to waqf officials and Christian leaders regarding their respective holy places.

The *fourth lesson* requires us to recognize that freedom of worship is only abstract unless *access* is provided to the holy places for worship. The issue is not who owns, or has historic worship rights to, a particular holy place, but rather how the holy places can be administered so as to provide public access while respecting community traditions, causing the least offense to any group and insuring safety and security.

An example of these difficulties can be seen in the problem of access to Jerusalem itself—because if a group does not have access to Jerusalem, the question of access to the holy places does not arise. As Jerusalem is considered part of Israel proper rather than part of the West Bank, closure of the territories for security reasons (or, as Palestinians claim, as punishment) has a significant effect on both Muslim and Arab Christian access to their holy sites.

On Easter 1996, for example, West Bank Palestinians were forbidden entry to Jerusalem for "security reasons" and Palestinian children could not participate in the "traditional Palm Sunday march by Palestinian boy and girl scouts."[5] In August 1997, 2,000 Greek Orthodox Christians from Bethlehem, Bayt Jala, and Bayt Sahur prayed at the Gilo checkpoint on the outskirts of Jerusalem when they were denied entry to the city to commemorate the festival of the Virgin Mary at

---

[4]   Ruth Lapidoth, "Jerusalem—Some Jurisprudential Aspects," *Catholic University Law Review* 45 (1996), p. 661.

[5]   Patrick Cockburn, "Patriarch Calls on Israel to 'Let my People Go,'" *Independent* (London), April 8, 1996, p. 9; see also Michael Jansen, "Jerusalem Ceremonies are Ruled Out for Palestinian Christians," *Irish Times*, April 8, 1996, p. 11.

the church named after her in Jerusalem.[6] And in 1996 and 1997, the Israeli army limited the number of Muslims it allowed to pray at Jerusalem holy sites on Friday during Ramadan, admitting them only if they already bore entrance permits to Israel and were more than thirty years old.[7] In 1998, in large part because of the intervention of Sephardic Chief Rabbi Bakshi-Doron, the Israeli government relaxed its criteria for entry of Palestinians into Jerusalem over Ramadan for prayer at the Haram. More than 275,000 worshipers were allowed access to the Haram for prayer on the last Friday of Ramadan this year (January 23, 1998).[8]

Such efforts to ensure security while allowing physical access to the holy places should be an important goal for Israel. They might, for example, include joint coordination with the Christian Churches to undertake security searches outside Jerusalem with the provision of special buses that travel directly to the churches. This approach was in fact suggested in Easter 1995 when Israel, after closing off the West Bank, offered to bus in Arab Christians for prayers.[9] Recently, both chief rabbis met with the Latin patriarch and one can only hope this will lead to improved access for Palestinian Christians to Christian holy places.[10] Already this spring, some 12,000 Palestinian Christians were allowed to visit Nazareth and Jerusalem for the Feast of the Annunciation. Security considerations need not require closure of holy places to worshipers.

The *fifth lesson* is both easy to state and hard to follow—resist the hallowing of new "holy places" whenever possible. The question of how various geographic sites become sanctified or vested with holiness is a complex issue that we cannot here resolve. The process, however, can be encouraged or retarded by political and economic decisions as well as by religious interpretation. Michael Dumper has pointed out how world Muslim interest in the Islamic holy places intensified after the June 1967 War.[11] Most recently we have seen the grave site of Baruch

---

[6] "Israeli Army Stops Palestinian Christians from Praying in Jerusalem," *BBC Summary of World Broadcasts,* August 30, 1997.

[7] "Israel Curbs Entrance to Palestinians," *Reuters*, February 9, 1996.

[8] Conversation with Rabbi Michael Melchior, Washington D.C., March 31, 1998.

[9] In March 1993 "some Palestinians were allowed to travel by bus from the West Bank directly and only to the Haram as-Sharif (where the al-Aqsa and Dome of the Rock mosques are located), [but] authorities often restricted access by male worshipers under a certain age." See section on "Occupied Territories" in *State Department Country Reports on Human Rights Practices for 1993* (Washington, D.C.: Department of State, 1994), pp. 1201–1210.

[10] Haim Shapiro, "Latin Patriarch's First Ever Visit Follows Year of Discussions. Sabah Meets Chief Rabbis," *Jerusalem Post*, March 24, 1998, p. 5.

[11] "An important counterpoint to the "Israelization" of Jerusalem is the revival of interest in the Islamic sites of the Old City of Jerusalem." Michael Dumper, *Israel and Islam: Muslim Religious Endowments and the Jewish State* (Washington, D.C.: Institute for Palestinian Studies, 1994), p. 104. Daniel Pipes has gone further, stating "Jerusalem has mattered to Muslims only intermittently over the past thirteen centuries, and when it has mattered, as it does today, it has been because of politics." Daniel Pipes, "If I forget thee," *New Republic,* April 28, 1997, p. 17.

Goldstein in Kiryat Arba begin to be "sacralized" and become a place for pilgrimage. Similarly, in certain nationalistic circles, the Grave of Joseph (Kever Yosef) in Nablus has begun to achieve a religious importance that it did not have in the past. It will be interesting to consider whether the recent discovery of a rock, believed to have been the resting place of Mary on her journey to Bethlehem, will create new "sacred space" as Christianity's "Jubilee" celebrations approach in the year 2000.[12] As Gideon Avni, Israel's chief archeologist for Jerusalem, has commented, "every stone we move here causes its own problems."[13]

The *sixth lesson* is one of clarity regarding the geographic boundaries of what in Hebrew one would call the *kedusha*—the holiness—of Jerusalem for each of the three monotheistic faiths. Does, for example, the kedusha of Jerusalem for Jews lie in the 1967 boundaries or in the Jewish Quarter of the Old City? What do Christians require to satisfy their need for "witness" in the holy land? What portions of Jerusalem are holy from an Islamic perspective? Such an exercise for each of the monotheistic faiths might prove instructive and should be undertaken with the unofficial support of the Israeli government.

The *seventh lesson* is that mechanisms, both formal and informal, must be structured to allow Israel to meet with the religious leadership of the major faiths on the basis of dignity and equality. At present, meetings with local representatives of the various religious faiths occur in piecemeal fashion with different ministries, notwithstanding the practical and unforeseen complications that ensue.[14] Only in the last year have Israel's chief rabbis begun to meet with their Christian and Muslim counterparts—and in so doing, have opened new informal channels of communication. These informal meetings should be encouraged.

In addition, the creation of separate Muslim and Christian interreligious councils that could meet with both the Rabbinic authorities and the government on matters of concern to each religious community would be useful and constructive. (For the Catholic Church, of course, such meetings must occur within the framework of the Fundamental Accord.) The Christian communities are likely to agree, albeit reluctantly (as they would rather quarrel in private than in front of the Israelis). Still, none of them want to lose the seat at the table that such a council would provide. Although the Muslims might well reject such offers as in some way legitimizing Israeli control in Jerusalem, Israel would be wise to make these offers repeatedly.

---

[12] Elaine Ruth Fletcher,"Legendary Rock Found on Mary's Path to Bethlehem," *Washington Post,* November 22, 1997, p. G12. Although the land on which the rock is located has received the blessing of the Orthodox patriarch of Jerusalem, the site has neither been opened to tourists nor has funding been found for preservation and exposition.

[13] Rebecca Trounson, "Where the Search for Relics is a Battlefield," *Los Angeles Times,* October 31, 1996, p. A1.

[14] See text above, p. 24, note 35.

In this regard, the celebration of the start of the third millennium of the Christian era, or "Jubilee year," in the year 2000 is an important moment for deepening Israeli–Christian contacts. In particular, the Jubilee is yet another opportunity to create coordinating structures among Christian denominations that can be used for other purposes as well. The Israeli government should take advantage of the large number of Christian pilgrims who are expected to visit Israel during the "Jubilee" year to help the Christian communities develop a coherent position.[15]

This is not simply a matter of political tactics. There is a practical need for such a mechanism. In April 1997, while building a toilet complex at the al-Khanga mosque near the Church of the Holy Sepulchre, waqf employees broke through a common wall with an adjoining church belonging to the Greek Patriarchate and walled up two rooms inhabited by a monk who was out of the country. Christian authorities met with Israeli Prime Minister Binyamin Netanyahu seeking assistance. Netanyahu urged the Muslims and Christians to work it out. Yet the Jerusalem district court issued an injunction at the request of the city claiming that the construction work was undertaken without a permit. Throughout this dispute, Catholics, Muslims, and Jews had no forum within which to speak and negotiate. Indeed, the lack of such a forum provided Jordan the opportunity to send envoys to mediate what is otherwise an eastern Jerusalem land conflict.[16]

This suggests that Israel should not completely ignore Jordanian interests in the holy places. As Israel and the Palestinians move toward final status negotiations, Amman's interest in representing the spiritual interest of Islam becomes significant. It serves to separate the Palestinian interest in physical sovereignty from the broader Arab interest in spiritual involvement in the holy city. Thus, bringing Jordan into the picture may make the sovereignty debate over the Temple Mount easier to handle.

The *eighth lesson* is one drawn from international law. Israel need not wait for a comprehensive settlement to move forward to improve its political and

---

[15] Larry Witham, "Holy Land Visits Seen Ballooning Next 3 Years," *Washington Times*, October 12, 1997, p. A5.

[16] As compensation the Jordanians offered the Greek Orthodox control of a church in southern Jordan that had been previously awarded to Muslims. For accounts of this contretemps see Haim Shapiro, "Christian–Moslem Dispute Escalates," *Jerusalem Post*, May 1, 1997, p. 3; Haim Shapiro, "*Waqf* Breaks into Greek Patriarchate, Seals Off Two Rooms," *Jerusalem Post*, April 13, 1997, p. 1; Laurie Copans, "Mosque takes over rooms outside Jerusalem's Church of Holy Sepulchre," *Agence France Press*, April 14, 1997; "Israeli PM to help resolve Christian–Muslim Dispute," *Reuters, North American Wire*, April 24, 1997; and "Jordan intervenes in Moslem–Christian Church Dispute in Jerusalem," *Agence France Press*, June 26, 1997.

As should be expected, the Jordanians, while claiming to have solved the problem "amicably," explicitly denied any geographical trade. "Jordan 'resolves' Muslim–Christian Dispute in Jerusalem," *Jordan Times (Associated Press)*, June 28, 1997, p. 2.

moral agenda regarding the holy places. Unlike traditional contract law, Israel may, under international law, enter into unilateral commitments that have a binding effect under international law when such commitments are made with the intention of creating international obligations.[17] Such an approach would track recent desires of the Vatican for Israeli guarantees for the protection of the holy places.[18] In this regard, the experience of the Greek churches on Mt. Athos may prove particularly relevant.

The *ninth lesson* necessitates the waqf taking special efforts to ensure that the Haram, as a sacred space, is not used to incite violence. Shortly after Jerusalem's reunification, Israel made an abortive effort to review the text of the Friday prayer sermons delivered on the Haram but was rebuffed. It wisely chose not to pursue the matter.[19] Waqf officials need to exercise parallel self-restraint and refrain from using religious services to stir violence, as they often did during the intifada and have continued to do, at times, in the post-Oslo era. The July 1997 sermon in al-Aqsa by Palestinian-appointed *mufti* Ikrama Sabri, in which Israeli settlers were branded "sons of monkeys and pigs," is an example of such inflammatory rhetoric.[20]

At the same time, the PA should refrain from the kind of dangerous language used by Chairman Arafat when he spoke to the Islamic Conference Summit in Tehran on December 10, 1997, and said, "I am ringing the bell of danger to warn against the Jewish plan to build the Temple of Solomon, in the place where today stands al-Aqsa Mosque, after removing the mosque. . ."[21] One cannot imagine comments more likely to thrust the region into convulsion. Moreover, the use of sacred symbols for violent purposes is sadly not limited to one side in this dispute. In late 1997, Israeli police arrested two Jewish militants for allegedly planning to catapult a pig's head with a Qur'an stuffed into its mouth onto the Haram—with the specific hope of causing a violent reaction.[22]

The PA should agree to preclude any individual from concurrently holding the positions of head of the Supreme Muslim Council and PA minister of religious affairs. However much Minister Hassan Tahboub may or may not

---

[17] See text above, p. 66 and footnote 34.

[18] See text above, pp. 31–35.

[19] Meron Benvenisti, in *City of Stone: The Hidden History of Jerusalem* (Berkeley: University of California Press, 1996), pp. 102–103, describes Muslim rejection of the Israeli effort to review religious sermons in advance. See also Meron Benvenisti, *Jerusalem: The Torn City* (Minneapolis: University of Minnesota Press, 1976), p. 284.

[20] See Jay Bushinsky, "Arafat-Appointed Mufti Calls Settlers 'Sons of Monkeys and Pigs,'" *Jerusalem Post*, July 14, 1997, p. 2.

[21] Idem., "'Israel planning to remove Aksa mosque,'" *Jerusalem Post International Edition*, December 20, 1997, p. 8.

[22] Elli Wohlgelernter, "Right Wing extremists arrested," *Jerusalem Post*, December 22, 1997, p. 2; "Police: Jewish extremists planned to throw pig onto Temple Mount," *Deutsche Presse-Agentur*, December 26, 1997.

attempt to distinguish his roles, it is structurally impossible for anyone holding both jobs not to be perceived by both Palestinians and Israelis as acting in violation of Israeli law regarding PA political activity in Jerusalem.

Finally, the *tenth lesson* is one that recognizes that the Christian communities seem unable to act in a joint manner except in very unusual circumstances. Consider, as a recent example, the wrangles over repairs to the Church of the Holy Sepulchre. The Christian communities need to clarify their goals in a concrete manner to present a more united voice. Although other religious communities lack the political character of the Vatican, the potentially beneficial character of the bilateral Fundamental Accord suggests the value of seeking foundational agreements with other Christian churches resident in the Holy Land. Such an agreement would be beneficial, certainly concerning issues of legal personality, tax exemption, and rights of access and recognition where appropriate. Agreement on practical issues such as repairs, sanitation, and upkeep for the various holy places can only lead to the kind of working arrangements urged in lesson seven.

CONCLUSION

The holy places lie at the intersection of religion and politics, at the symbolic cusp of sacred geography. They may be among the most difficult of the issues to resolve in any "final" settlement. Indeed, a recent survey of Palestinian opinion has suggested that 94 percent of those surveyed view the Haram as "very important as part of [their] Jerusalem";[23] 93 percent of Jews surveyed held similar views regarding the Temple Mount.[24] Wending one's way between these polar views will require patience, if not Solomonic wisdom.

This monograph is but a preliminary guide to the issues surrounding the holy places, providing some suggestions as how to deal with them. As the peace process proceeds, however fitfully, these issues will begin to dominate the horizon. If they are to be successfully managed—let alone solved—sensitivity to history, religious doctrine, and religious symbolism will be essential. We can only hope that the sensitivity that has been lacking by all parties in recent years will reemerge as final status talks draw near.

---

[23] Nader Izzat Said and Jerome M. Segal, *The Status of Jerusalem in the Eyes of Palestinians* (College Park: University of Maryland, Center of International and Security Studies, June 1997), p. 130 (Table 9).

[24] Elihu Katz and Shlomit Levy, *The Status of Jerusalem in The Eyes of Israeli Jews* (College Park: University of Maryland, Center of International and Security Studies, January 1997). Other researchers from the Jerusalem Institute of Israel Studies have found that "93% of Israelis think that the Temple Mount is important, 86% want to be able to worship there and 70% oppose formalizing the Islamic Trust's status at the site." See "Researchers Warn Against Changing Status Quo on Temple Mount," *Jerusalem Post*, July 10, 1997, p. 16.